C000172385

SEEKING THE SCALLOP SHELL

SEEKING THE SCALLOP SHELL

Marilyn Parkes-Seddon

ARTHUR H. STOCKWELL LTD
Torrs Park, Ilfracombe, Devon, EX34 8BA
Established 1898
www.ahstockwell.co.uk

British Library Cataloguing-in-Publication Data.
A catalogue record for this book is available
from the British Library.

Arthur H. Stockwell Ltd bears no responsibility
for the accuracy of information recorded in this book.

By the same author:
The Jonquil

ISBN 978-0-7223-5005-8
Printed in Great Britain by
Arthur H. Stockwell Ltd
Torrs Park   Ilfracombe
Devon EX34 8BA

DEDICATION

In memory of my parents, Samuel and Doris Parkes.

ACKNOWLEDGEMENTS

With thanks to Sean Webb for his original line drawings, which accompany each chapter; my friend Valerie Blake, for her beautiful calligraphy; and my unpaid PA (actually my husband, Malc), for his unfailing encouragement and support. Also to my friends and family, whose support has provided much needed encouragement.

Many thanks go to all the people I met during my many pilgrimages. The added knowledge and detail they provided proved intrinsic to the book.

A special thanks to Mark Boyling, Dean of Carlisle Cathedral, for his willingness to put his endorsement to my book; it means a lot.

Original pen-and-ink drawings by Sean Webb. For commissions contact: webbsean@btinternet.com.

Photographs by Malcolm Seddon.

CONTENTS

FOREWORD

by

the Very Reverend Mark Boyling, Dean of Carlisle Cathedral

If you think that pilgrimage is a minority interest in our twenty-first century, think again! More than 300,000 people completed the Camino de Santiago in 2018; in our own country, more than 250,000 pilgrims visit the shrine at Walsingham each year; and if we think about other world faiths, 2 million people began the annual hajj pilgrimage to Mecca in 2019.

So pilgrimage is alive and well. For some the religious motivation remains very clear and many would say that the commitment to use this time to draw near to God bears important fruit. For others, without any explicit religious faith, the time spent on pilgrimage often gives space for reflection and reorientation in the midst of the changes and chances of life.

Marilyn's book introduces us to twenty-two pilgrimage sites in the UK – a good number of those being in the north of the country. From her home in the Borders, she visited them all over a two-year period and she sets out the experience of those visits together with her immediate impressions. She adds, in a very accessible way, the research and reflections her visits have prompted.

Perhaps her book will prompt us to include these sites on any journey we make – be it long or short, on foot or by car. We are left in no doubt that these are special places where people have found themselves close to God.

INTRODUCTION

Scallops today are a popular shellfish and in many parts of Scotland, and indeed elsewhere, they are a sought-after catch for fishermen.

In Kirkudbright, a lovely town in Dumfries and Galloway, the scallop is the specialism of the few trawlermen who sail out of this once much busier port. It has proved a lucrative substitute for fish other no longer caught. When Malc and I once visited we watched the return of a couple of trawlers which had been out at sea for several days and were returning with a successful large catch, ready chilled in their boxes, waiting to be unloaded. We stood at the port side along with families and children, awaiting their husbands' return. Like fishing traditions of old, there is still hazard to this occupation, families standing hopeful of the fishermen's safe return.

Yet scallop shells have an old and different tradition, one spread across Europe, beginning it is believed with the shrine of St James at Santiago of Compostela, and the scallop shell is still very much associated with this popular pilgrim site today. It is indeed an old Christian symbol. St James is said to have arrived in Spain in AD 44. The scallop shell is said to have originated in Galicia, the North Spanish area where St James's Pilgrim Way is situated. Additionally, the raised lines on the scallop shell were, and still are, meant to represent the various paths taken by pilgrims, where all paths and people come together: firstly at the shrine, but also the convergence with Jesus, as the centre of our lives. In this way life itself is a pilgrimage, seeking spiritual meaning and finding our way through life. The idea of the scallop shell as a mark of pilgrimage grew and spread. Perhaps people returned from a Spanish pilgrimage and brought their scallop shells home, helping to spread the symbolism. Even though some UK pilgrim sites had their own badges, nevertheless the scallop shell remained the universally recognised symbol of a pilgrim.

The image was found on badges, clothes and books, in churches and at shrines, a representation of those people who travelled on spiritual pilgrimages to many places and in many countries. Pilgrimages to holy places and shrines, mostly of esteemed and venerated saints, were extremely popular activities. There was no shortage of places to go and no shortage of pilgrims to travel there. People from all classes, regions and occupations wanted to experience at least one pilgrimage. It was equally likely to see kings and queens and nobles alongside peasants and artisans.

In these twenty-first-century times, when the country is considerably more secular than religious, today it may seem a strange thing to want to go on a pilgrimage to revere a long-dead saint. But in past times it did not appear odd. In fact, it was a normal, natural and exciting thing to do. It was the ambition of the majority of people. In the Middle Ages in particular, religion was an integral part of people's lives and most would have had a fervent faith, church attendance a normal and expected part of everyday activity. This belief influenced people's everyday thoughts, actions and understanding of life and the society they lived in. This is understandable when realising that the Church had an overwhelming presence and influence. Most would profess to being believers and worshippers, and the Church and its clergy were as integral as the local inn, feast and festival days, family and tradition.

At a time without clocks, the church was a village timekeeper, its bells ringing out the hours and telling people it was time to leave their tasks for worship. Marriage and baptism were important, and the Church was the only institution to offer both, and of course the Church buried the village dead. Nor was this observance purely show. People's beliefs were strong, believing strongly in purgatory. They longed for heaven. Death was an ever present fact. Heaven meant an afterlife, which was very real to them. But sins committed on earth in their lifetime warned of the real possibility of being in purgatory, which is neither heaven nor hell, where they were judged, their very soul at risk of never reaching heaven. Repentance, good deeds and pilgrimage were all ways of building a 'good' life and the increased chance of entering heaven.

The Church then – at that time, of course, the only Church being that of Rome – had a powerful hold over people and their lives.

I thought it would be an interesting project to look at the history of, and experience of, pilgrimage. But, more than being just an historical study, I took it further by visiting both old and modern centres of pilgrimage. It has been and was intended to be a spiritual journey and to experience what was such an important aspect of life more than 1,000 years ago.

It has, however, proved to be much more than this. My husband, Malc, and I went together over a period of over two years to visit twenty-two different shrines across the UK. These journeys took me to many different beautiful and interesting places. Geography, nature, history, people and landscape proved equally important, providing a much more holistic approach to the shrine itself. Each shrine, saint and building had a different story to tell. The UK, despite its small size, has an immense variety of interesting things and places. The end result is a travelogue where pilgrimage and spirituality is the focus and vehicle in the context of a modern Britain with its infinite expression of heritage, beauty and interesting people.

This 'odyssey' proved to be far more interesting than I could ever have imagined, as well as being challenging, exciting and thought-provoking, taking me to places I probably wouldn't otherwise have gone. An eye-opening experience, and I hope it will be for you too.

A pilgrimage prayer by Sir Walter Raleigh
Give me my scallop shell of quiet
My staff of faith to walk upon
My skript of joy, immortal diet
My bottle of salvation
My gown of glory, hopes true gauge
And this I'll take my pilgrimage

ST KENTIGERN AND THE BEGINNINGS OF GLASGOW

The city of Glasgow and its surrounding hinterland of other towns is the largest conurbation in Scotland. With its rich industrial heritage, famous museums and people, it is easy to forget that Glasgow was once a tiny town by the banks of the Molendinar Burn. The importance of the River Clyde and its port was an altogether later trigger for urban and industrial development. Glasgow was probably a village as early as the sixth century, reputedly established by St Kentigern, who is the city's patron saint. The Glasgow coat of arms reflects this. Many of the symbols represent elements from the life of Kentigern, also known as Mungo. How authentic the stories are is, however, hard to know.

What we do know of Kentigern is little indeed. The only certain fact is his date of death, in AD 617. Other supposed facts about his life are probably apocryphal, although his upbringing in the lovely Fife village of Culross may be true. The possibility that he was of noble birth is also not dismissed out of hand. Certainly, Culross, on the Forth Estuary, has a long ecclesiastic history; it was the residence of St Serf, who is reputed to have run a school for boys here. So it is possible that Kentigern was raised and protected there by St Serf. Kentigern, however, was destined to leave the village's safety and seclusion, and as a young adult we know he wandered around the country in what we now call Scotland's central belt. He eventually came to rest at the spot by the Molendinar Burn, and here he stayed. This was part of the large and powerful Kingdom of Strathclyde, its base being Dumbarton.

Kentigern is reputed to have known and been friends with the King. It was here he stayed, preaching, baptising and attracting people to him, so that this area grew, developed and eventually became the city of Glasgow. A church grew and Kentigern became bishop of this huge area. His reputation and following was so great that he eventually built a cathedral on this spot. The current cathedral stands in this same place. There has been some debate, though, since no artefacts or remains from Kentigern's time have been found here, and some historians have considered an ancient ecclesiastic site in Govan as Kentigern's initial base. Whether or not this is true, the cathedral must at some point have moved to its current position. The church and bishopric begun by Kentigern grew and prospered and became Glasgow Cathedral.

So Malc and I went in search of St Kentigern. It was an easy journey for us: only one hour by train from Lockerbie, a journey undertaken every day by many commuters. It was a nondescript, grey, chilly day, but dry, and our walk from the railway station to the cathedral was unhurried. Being a cathedral, we had anticipated a fairly short walk. We followed the signs and carried on walking until we felt that we had either missed it or taken the wrong road. It seemed to be an awfully long way. We had left the city throngs behind us, passed the university, and we were still onward travellers.

"This can't be right," I said to Malc as we stopped and tried to get our bearings. "We must have come too far. Perhaps we should turn back. What do you think, Malc?"

"I don't know. You're right though it doesn't seem right, but we followed all the signs. Shall I ask someone?"

"Go on, then," I agreed, feeling a little foolish, not being able to find such a prominent city landmark.

"Excuse me," Malc said politely as he approached what looked like a student. "We're looking for the cathedral. Are we near it?"

"Aye" came the reply. "Just carry on to the bottom of this street and you can't miss it."

"Thank you," we both said.

We carried on, and in a couple of hundred yards there it was.

Glasgow Cathedral is a rare Scottish survivor from pre-Reformation times, and what luck that it wasn't destroyed! It is old and beautiful. It is a wonderful place to visit if only because, unlike England, Scotland has few remaining cathedrals and these are in name only. The Scottish Reformation, opposed to pomp and with its dislike of bishops and Church hierarchy, led the movement for change. Presbyterianism, with its flat structure, control from the centre moving to local people, became the official creed of the Church of Scotland. Cathedrals with their inherent bishoprics ceased to exist. Glasgow's cathedral only survived because it was divided into three separate worship areas and allocated to the Church of Scotland congregations. It still serves a Church of Scotland congregation today, but as one, not three. The fabric of the church is cared for by Historic Scotland. There is nothing remaining of Kentigern's church, the current cathedral having been mostly built in the thirteenth century, and it is recognised as a fine example of this period, with wonderful Gothic detail. Yet Kentigern does have a presence here still, for his tomb lies in the crypt.

This is an older part of the church, with parts dating back to the 1100s. There is some beautiful ribbed vaulting here, and the area around the tomb appears to have a layout which emphasises it, yet also encloses it as if to protect the precious relics within. In general, it is a simple unostentatious but quiet and reverent place in which to remember Glasgow's special saint.

Before entering the cathedral one thing struck me as strange, remembering our long walk to get there. The cathedral today stands outside and beyond what would be regarded as the heart of Glasgow. Having visited many cathedrals, they always seem to be an integral part of the city in which they stand, also contributing wholeheartedly to the city's identity and character. Even when not absolutely in the middle of the city, sometimes becoming a little off-centre as the city develops and grows, cathedrals nevertheless generally still remain part of the city, recognised and used by residents and visitors alike. At Carlisle Cathedral, where we worship, people use the cathedral close as a summer picnic spot, a walk-through as a shortcut to other streets, a sitting and relaxing space. It belongs to its people. Glasgow doesn't follow this pattern. A large city, which has changed and spread, Glasgow's heartland lies elsewhere. Whilst the cathedral is old, beautiful and majestic, it also seems forlorn and almost abandoned in its own city. There is no sense of it being integral to Glasgow's heritage and certainly not to the modern city. The area in which it stands has been upgraded and is pleasant and attractive, including its close neighbour, which is the city's oldest building. But it has lost something. Its meaning? Its identity? Clearly it is a wonderful survivor, with beautiful architecture and a vibrant history, but to me it seemed to stand more as a memorial rather than as a living, breathing testament in its relationship to the city, though it owes its existence to a man centuries ago who came here, stayed and spawned a city.

Yet there was a time, of course, when this church was a magnet for pilgrims coming to honour and worship at St Kentigern's shrine. Surprisingly, the shrine was not located in the crypt, by his tomb. Rather a separate shrine was established within the body of the church, especially to accommodate pilgrims. We know that this shrine existed in 1301 because King Edward I of England visited and paid homage at both the shrine and his tomb. Although a shrine by his tomb would have been the most logical thing, it was felt that it would have been difficult to make it pilgrim-friendly. A very elaborate shrine was therefore built up on the floor of the nave. It would appear to have been elaborate – a stone base and a golden vaulted roof. It was built in what is termed a feretory, this being a shrine chapel – a space specially set aside with aisles and decorative screens, a place where pilgrims could rest, pray and worship in front of the shrine in relative privacy from the rest of the church. In reality, this privacy was illusory, so many pilgrims queued outside the area, creating an atmosphere of great excitement and anticipation, perhaps a little agitated, wanting to move along so they could enter. What happened to the shrine and when isn't known, but, like so many others, it has been destroyed and lost to history.

Some questions occurred to me. If Kentigern's remains were in the tomb in the crypt, what was in the shrine? If there were relics, what and whose were they? If none, did the pilgrims know they were worshipping at an empty shrine? Did they accept that this only represented Kentigern, but still believed that his presence could be discerned here? At a time of fervent faith, belief could and did accept many things. God was everywhere. His saints, who represented Him, could in many miraculous ways be present wherever they were needed.

During our visit, a choir was practising for a performance. There seemed to be many activities indicating a lively church, but there were no pilgrims other than Malc and me. It was hard to imagine the hordes of people who once came here. We are used to churches being quiet places, but in those medieval times Glasgow Cathedral was busy, noisy, overflowing with faith and deep gratitude towards Kentigern, the man of great faith and the founder of what would become a great city.

By now it was time for a cup of tea. We left and walked back towards the city centre and found ourselves in Sauchiehall Street and the Willow Tea Rooms. These were the creation of another famous Scot, Charles Rennie Mackintosh, whose characteristic architectural style is now world-famous. His flowing and also stylised art nouveau patterns are unmistakable. The Willow Tea Rooms were designed by him, and now on partaking of a cup of tea it is possible to look at and admire his designs, from chairs to windows. It is as fresh and authentic as it was when it was first done. Many people think his work was vast, but the opposite is true. He was not overly popular at the time. His designs were striking, unusual and unique, and it was only forward-thinkers who were able to appreciate what he was doing. He received few commissions. The famous Glasgow School of Art, designed by him, now acclaimed and sadly recently burned down, was hated by many, and Mackintosh was not even invited to the official opening. Of his few admirers, we must be grateful to the owner of Hillhouse in Helensburgh, a town along the Clyde Estuary, who commissioned the whole house to be designed inside by Charles Rennie Mackintosh. The owner of Hillhouse was the owner of Blackie's, a publisher, and he was rich. Over time he could have altered his house as styles changed. He didn't. Hillhouse is a time capsule dedicated to the memory and talent of Charles Rennie Mackintosh, and it is a fortunate survivor, allowing us to enjoy seeing it today as it was in the original untouched style.

He may not have been successful in his time, but today he is an international style icon.

Kentigern was a popular worshipped and revered man and saint for hundreds of years during the Middle Ages, and yet now he is a distant memory. Whilst people know of Charles Rennie Mackintosh, who now really reveres St Kentigern? But, then, he did live a long time ago. Yet Glaswegians remember that without beloved Kentigern there might never have been a Glasgow!

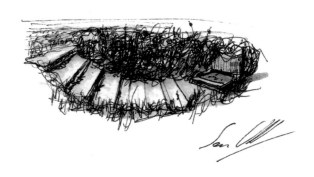

ST KENTIGERN IN CUMBRIA

Caldbeck in North Cumbria is most famous as the village of John Peel, the local huntsman immortalised in the famous 'D'ye ken John Peel with his coat so grey?' Yet in this lovely village there are far more ancient traditions, and Malc and I had come to the parish church not to find John Peel's grave in the churchyard, but to find St Kentigern, who stayed and preached here. The church, named after him, was built somewhat later than the sixth century, having a beginning in the twelfth. It is almost certain, however, that some earlier church, probably of wood, was built as early as the 600s.

We met Kentigern previously in Glasgow. It was on a journey south that he stayed here before moving on to other places, both in Cumbria and possibly as far south as Wales, after which he returned to Glasgow.

Caldbeck today is still a small, quiet and beautiful village, unspoilt and still relatively untouched by modern development. Today's peaceful scene, however, belies its history of mills and breweries. The Cald Beck, which runs through the village along with other smaller tributaries, was perfect for the local watermill. It can be a busy place for visitors, but on a cool autumn day, the earlier sun and blue sky having retreated into dark clouds, we were virtually the only visitors. We strolled down quiet lanes and over bridges, the beck below bubbling and gurgling along its course. What remained of autumn colour was lovely, but most leaves had fallen. It still allowed for an autumn walk with dry fallen leaves crunching under our feet.

This is the Lake District, or at least it is the Lake District National Park. Yet vast tracts of the park are barely trodden compared to the major centres around Keswick and Windermere.

We walked through the church gates following a long straight path through the churchyard up to the church, one which is open every day when so many are permanently locked. There were yew trees here, one with masses of scarlet berries. We also walked in between two shaped yew trees standing proudly beside the path. Yew is often called the churchyard tree, where they are still often seen today. For thousands of years it has been regarded as a sacred tree, for pagan Celts and later Christians too. It is an extremely long-lived tree, evergreen, representing everlasting life, and is a 'tree of protection'.

I remember some years ago Malc and I were on holiday in Perthshire. We had treated ourselves to a Highland off-road safari run by a company based in Dull. The safari itself was advertised as 'Dull Highland Tours'. No, not a joke – look it up yourself. It is still operating! In fact, making the most of its name, the village has recently been twinned with the town called Boring in Australia and another called Bland in the USA!

Anyway, close to Dull is a famous tree, the Fortingall Yew, and it is quite astounding. It is reckoned to be the oldest tree in Britain, the rest of Europe and possibly the world, at 5,000 years old. It is hard to imagine that before Jesus was born, before the Romans conquered the known world, even before men in Britain forged iron, this tree was already growing in Perthshire's remote hills. When we visited, its trunk, though supported, was clearly still alive. There again, we would certainly need support at 5,000 years old!

Now back to Caldbeck Church. The beauty inside testifies to its age and I was particularly interested in a stained-glass window dedicated to both St Kentigern and St Cuthbert, with lovely authentic impressions of both. I found it surprising that everywhere I went on my visits the same people and saints crop up. It seems that Cuthbert too came here, but it is understandable on realising that this area was part of the great Anglian Northumberland kingdom. Whether King Oswald was with him isn't known.

What I had really come to Caldbeck to see was St Kentigern's Well. The Cald Beck runs right behind the church, and we took the footpath over the ancient packhorse bridge in the oldest part of the village. The well, which we thought was by this river, wasn't immediately visible, but by looking from the bridge up and down the riverbanks we saw it. There were a few shallow steps down from the riverside path, at the bottom of which was the well. Modest, and almost hidden by undergrowth, nevertheless its size does not reflect its importance in respect of early Christian history.

Across Britain there are still many healing wells, many in almost forgotten remote spots, where the water was recognised as possessing special healing properties. Often this was because certain mineral elements were contained in the water. Over time, spas were developed, and Bath, Buxton and Leamington Spa were amongst many others where it became the place to be. Flourishing purely because of this special water, harnessed from local springs, these new fashionable places attracted gentry in their droves.

Holy wells, of which again there used to be many, were slightly different. Yes, these too were believed to have healing qualities, but it was not because of the water itself (though there were often special properties in it). Rather, its specialness was because it had been endowed with the power of a saint. St Kentigern's Well is purportedly where he preached and then used the well water to baptise. This was still a predominantly pagan area, but Kentigern attracted crowds of people, who came to listen to him and went on to adopt the Christian faith and become baptised members of it. Its association with Kentigern remained long after he left the area. People continued to recognise the well's special powers, so it continued as a well of healing and Christian faith.

We walked down the few short steps and found the small well still clearly delineated by a shallowish rectangular stone bath.

The water it contained was clear and could be seen bubbling up from a small underground spring. Dipping our hands into the water we found it cool, but not freezing cold as we would have expected on such a day.

It was time for the usual refreshments. We were the only customers in the Old Smithy Café and Ice-Cream Parlour, complete with an old anvil, which reminded us of the Gretna 'blacksmith weddings'. Malc fancied an ice cream, but declined on such a cold day. The owner told us the ice cream was made on the premises, the milk provided by village cows. We were particularly interested in a variety called 'Dairy Longhorn'.

"Is it really quiet at the moment?" I asked her, looking round at all the empty tables.

"More like dead," she answered. "No one seems to be coming in."

I could understand, as we noticed how deserted the village had been. I felt quite sorry for her, so asked her a bit about their ice cream. We promised to come back on a warm day and try some, and we will.

"You won't be disappointed," she emphasised as we left to go back to our car for the drive home.

It was getting dark and quite chilly, and we were glad of the warm car and the thought of home. We also talked about the Dairy Longhorn.

"You don't suppose they actually add the longhorn to it, do you?" I asked Malc.

Passing Gretna Green reminded me of John Peel.

"Did you know John Peel was married over the anvil at Gretna Green?" I asked Malc.

"I had heard that."

There were lots of other well-known people who married there, eloping in order to marry the person of their choice because of opposition from parents. James Goldsmith and his daughter years later married here, but that is a different story altogether.

ST KENTIGERN: AN EXILE AT HODDOM

On a beautiful afternoon in late summer Malc and I were visiting a pilgrim site close to my home in Annandale in the eastern part of Dumfries and Galloway. The dale is named after the lovely River Annan, a shortish river rising in Moffat to the north and flowing into the Solway Firth at Annan. It is nevertheless famous for both salmon and trout. Annan, at the river mouth, was once a very busy port where smuggling was endemic and where the famous Robert Burns, when not writing his poems, was employed by Customs and Excise. A few miles upriver from Annan is Hoddom, a popular spot on the riverbank for fishermen, more accustomed to spotting otters and kingfishers whilst waiting for the elusive bite, rather than searching out pilgrim sites. Most passers-by will probably not even be aware of the ancient historic spot hiding in the long grass beside the river.

St Kentigern (Mungo) lived here at what was, and still is, a remote, beautiful and peaceful place. The pilgrims are long gone, but when Kentigern was here it was a vibrant and exciting place to be. More famous as Mungo, the patron saint of Glasgow, he was a loved and revered man of God who brought many people to the Christian faith. When he was in Glasgow, in the seventh century, he at some point decided to travel, some saying he was exiled and went south at least as far as Rheged (modern Cumbria), if not further. But his heart was in his homeland and he eventually returned to Scotland. The reason why isn't known, but he rested at Hoddom and stayed for several years. People welcomed him, and his presence, spirituality and teaching drew more and more to him. Many thousands were apparently converted to the Christian faith as a result. Kentigern built a church here and then an abbey, reputedly of considerable size. The original church and abbey were lost, but subsequent churches nearby have retained the name of St Mungo.

Parking near the river, it is an easy walk to where Kentigern's abbey and church are believed to have been and where its footprint has been identified. A bridge over the river leads to a footpath through a farmer's field. Then, a few hundred yards on, you arrive at what is locally known as Kentigern's Graveyard. Also here are the abbey remains. Long grass hides this sacred place. Some specimen trees in the near distance indicate the spot. A little closer and a broken-down fence and rickety gate mark its boundary. What is quickly apparent is that this is not the original graveyard, but rather one dating from around the seventeenth century. It is an old and atmospheric churchyard nonetheless. The area has been left to do its own thing. Some paths had been beaten down between gravestones, some listing or prone, but some still upright and carved with interesting symbols: angels, heraldic badges, hourglasses. Many of these are as crisp as when they were first carved. With blue sky, droning bees, butterflies, damselflies and wild flowers, it is quiet and peaceful.

"What a lovely place!" I said to Malc. "We could be miles from anywhere."

Yet it is elsewhere in this small area where we need to look to find Kentigern, and indicators are few. The outline of his original church can just about be seen, and artificial mounds and dykes, deeper into the fields away from the river, highlight the boundaries to his abbey. Excavations some years ago uncovered stone crosses, possibly Anglian, from the eighth century. This part of South-West Scotland was, at the time, part of the Kingdom of Strathclyde, an Anglian stronghold with its base at Dumbarton Rock. This resonates with other similar-aged crosses in the area – especially the famous, rare and beautiful Ruthwell Cross, standing only a few miles west in Ruthwell Church, close to the Solway shore. Dumfries and Galloway has an abundance of such crosses, some of which are thought to be waymarkers and praying crosses to help pilgrims find their way. In such remote and often desolate places, without roads and with few people, finding your way was not easy. Although these crosses are mostly of a later date than Kentigern, it does indicate that this was an early Christian site. In addition to the peacefulness there is a certain special feel here, which seems to bear testament to its spirituality and the reverence of thousands of pilgrims who hundreds of years ago came to find Kentigern and listened and worshipped as he preached his Christian message.

For a small and lightly populated area, Annandale continued to develop as an important place in Scottish history, its borderland geography giving it a unique history. The Scottish Wars of Independence were often focused on this area, with the Solway as the backdrop. But not everyone will know that the hero of independence, Robert the Bruce, later King Robert, was Lord of Annandale. The remains of his motte and bailey on the banks of the River Annan still exist, and there is a well-known apocryphal story attached to Robert from the times of these wars. In the small village of Kirkpatrick-Fleming, a few miles from Annan, is the reputed Bruce's Cave. High above the Kirtlewater, a small local river, in a cleft in a cliff, lies the cave. In a leafy glade where the Kirtlewater meanders its way to Gretna and the Solway the cave is cleverly hidden. The story goes that Robert the Bruce was hiding from his enemies in this cave one day, and he was watching a spider desperately trying to spin a web and continually failing to do so. Yet the spider did not give up, but started again and again. As Robert watched, he is said to have gained inspiration, introducing the phrase 'If at first you don't succeed, try, try again.' This gave him encouragement. He left his cave to fight another day, leading to his successful battle against the English, and to being created king.

But back to Hoddom and Kentigern. The pilgrims may have gone, but they have been replaced by visitors of a different kind, seeking out solace in a tranquil spot. We returned up the footpath, pausing to look at the river – no salmon or trout jumping, but a few mallards gently gliding along. Back over the bridge, we followed a private road up to Hoddom Castle. There is little to Hoddom apart from the castle, so even today it doesn't look much different to how Kentigern would have seen it. The castle, once home to the area's famous Maxwell family, now comprises a large caravan and campsite in its grounds, so cleverly hidden it can barely be seen from the road. It is popular and provides a strange contrast. The twenty-first-century visitors in their caravans, tents, bothies and pods are not unlike the pilgrim campers of 1,500 years ago. We drove to the café, which was deserted.

"Quiet?" I asked as I paid for our cups of tea.

"Yes," replied the waitress. "We're coming up to the end of our season. We'll close up completely over the winter."

But on this still lovely day we took our tea outside and sat in the courtyard, where our only companion was an older man with his Border collie. Instead of tea, he was enjoying a Guinness, some of which he put in a saucer on the ground for his dog, which was lapping it up. I smiled, for he seemed to be enjoying sharing his master's drink.

"It's an unspoilt, lovely place this," I said to him.

He responded and told me he had a caravan here at Hoddom and had been coming for over thirty years. "It's a gorgeous place," he said.

I couldn't disagree. It most certainly is.

ST KENTIGERN AND MERLIN

There are many stories surrounding the life of Kentigern, all of which reflect his widespread ministry as well as his contact with many people in his missionary role. No story, however, can be stranger than that which links him with the magician Merlin, in the sixth century.

The romance of Arthur, Merlin and the Round Table is an all-pervading story of heroism, knights, magic and the rescue of the Celtic peoples from Saxon invaders. Of course we truthfully do not know whether these Arthurian tales are true. Whether Arthur, his knights and Merlin ever even existed, most people I feel would like to believe he was a real person. Most people too, not expert in Arthurian history, would almost certainly place Arthur and his legends in the south-west of England. Yet there are many other areas of Britain where folk tales and folk memories of both Arthur and Merlin have long pedigrees in believing them to be from much further north. Many places here in lowland Scotland, by place names and association, hint at distant memories. In the Scottish Borders there is a long and strong connection to these two famous celebrities of Dark Age Britain. There are many tantalising hints in place names, burial places and landmarks, and belief in Merlin's association with this area goes back a very long way.

The earliest reference to Merlin (also known as Myrddin) in this area dates back to the sixth century. A major story tells us that at the end of his life Merlin sought out Kentigern and asked to be baptised as a Christian. This event is reputed to have taken place near a small village called Stobo in Upper Tweedsdale, between Biggar and Peebles.

Kentigern probably already knew Merlin, probably by crossing paths in their joint homeland. Agreeing to the baptism, Kentigern used a convenient stone as an altar, still extant and reputedly of great age. Today most visitors to the area around Tweedsdale and Stobo associate it either with Stobo Castle, a famous if expensive spa, and the Dawyck Botanic Gardens close by with beautiful gardens which are part of the University of Edinburgh. Yet much earlier history is not forgotten here, and the link with Merlin remains strong; there is even a 'Merlin Trail'.

Upper Tweedsdale is a spectacularly beautiful area and Malc and I set off to find both Kentigern the saint and Merlin the magician on an early spring day. Tweedsdale, however, didn't seem to realise it was spring, and on the way we encountered a variety of weather: sleet, snowstorms and rain, with low menacing cloud obscuring the hilltops and the temperature dropping to half a degree! But, intrepid travellers that we are, this didn't faze us and we carried on regardless! We travelled up the M74 north and left it at the junction for Moffat. This is a lovely and popular small town, with many tourists stopping off here on their journey. One shop not to be missed here is the Moffat Toffee Shop, with its famous and unique Moffat toffee, which probably keeps many weary travellers going on their often long journeys.

From here we headed deep into the interior of high mountains, conifer plantations, thousands of sheep and very little else.

This is described as an alternative scenic route to Edinburgh and worth the detour from the motorway. This is empty countryside at its very best. The famous River Tweed has its source here, a sign proclaiming it, and parking spaces for people to see where this important and famous salmon river starts its life. Disappointingly, the source is underground here, though it soon emerges as a small trickle and can be followed on our road, seeing it steadily growing, widening, circling and meandering. The surrounding bleak hills belie this area's past, for in Merlin's time there was a huge forest here. It was exceedingly dense too, as well as being inhabited by wild animals such as bears and wolves; totally different to the tamer much more open forests of today. The forest known as the Celidon Forest stretched from England's border to the capital, Edinburgh, and here Merlin was reputed to live. He has been depicted as the typical wild man of the forest, where he supposedly lived for most of his adult life, alone, scavenging for food, but ultimately surviving in what he came to consider home. Kentigern knew this land well too. His travels in the area taught him its features as well as its dangers, and his journeys here brought him into contact with people whom he sought to convert to Christianity. Kentigern is generally associated with Glasgow, but he also travelled widely, and it is believed that this area of Upper Tweedsdale was important to him.

The small church at Stobo is very old; indeed it is believed to be one of Scotland's oldest churches. It stands on high ground, away from the road, and a commanding view can be seen by a short uphill stroll through the graveyard. The church, though small, is an amalgam of styles, dating back to at least the twelfth century. However, many believe it is considerably older and that a much earlier church was built on the same site by St Kentigern in the sixth century. So far no remains from this early date have been found.

Inside are many tantalising features and artefacts, testifying to its great age. There are ancient stones and grave covers (with more outside) on display in the north aisle. In the early twentieth century this aisle was in a ruinous state, but it was rebuilt in the 1920s. Many believe that this collapsed section of the church was where Kentigern's early church stood. The rebuilding of this aisle does indeed resemble a small Saxon chapel. Sadly, it is unlikely that this was his chapel. It may not be far away, but it hasn't yet been found.

Detail about Merlin is hard to find, but much of the folklore centres on his attendance, if not involvement, in the sixth century at the Battle of Arthuret. This is an ancient parish close to the modern town of Longtown, near Carlisle, and its name has led to much speculation about its association with Arthur, as it is a place that actually includes his name. This battle (the site now being in Cumbria) did not involve Arthur, but the battle itself is likely to be authentic.

The Dark Age kingdoms in these Northern British areas were often involved in battles, not just to counter the inroads of the Anglo-Saxons, but rather between the kings themselves. There were often power struggles between siblings too. The Battle of Arthuret was a bloody one, even though it may not have involved hordes of fighters. It is thought to have been fought in 573 between rival kings of Rheged, a large and powerful kingdom incorporating all of current Cumbria and much more.

Merlin is thought to have been a retainer knight or even advisor to one of these kings, but became horrified by the brutality of the battle. The noise, the blood and the violent spectacle were too much for him. Today we would probably say he was suffering from PTSD. As a result Merlin ran away into the huge Celidon Forest, from which he never returned. Merlin was a pagan, and one of the recurring theories about him is the possibility that he was a Druid. If so, he was one of the last remaining members of this Celtic caste.

Considered a powerful priestly class, Druids were believed to be the receptacles of knowledge, magic and arcane rituals, including sacrifice. They are represented as having long beards and long hair, with responsibility for certain sacred rituals. Many of these rituals included absolute reverence for trees, especially the oak, particularily when wreathed in mistletoe, a plant of the highest order. But there is only one contemporary written account of the ritual of cutting mistletoe with a golden sickle, and that is the one described by Pliny. What seems to be more certain is that their love of trees and forests meant that their worship was in small cleared glades rather than temples. Regarding this, the Romans were confused, unable to understand why such powerful men did not build physical structures for the worship of their gods.

The appearance of Merlin as a pagan, unkempt, living in the dense forest with a reputation as a magician and sage, certainly lends atmosphere if not truth to the idea that he was a Druid. He knew how to survive here and did so for many years. He was said to have been familiar with the King of Strathclyde, a Christian, with his base in the massive rock fortress of Dumbarton Rock, on the Clyde Estuary.

Similarly, Kentigern was also well acquainted with and loved by this Strathclyde king, and the Celidon Forest and the Kingdom of Strathclyde were among his regular and known stamping grounds. Over time the King, the pagan and the Christian missionary no doubt encountered one another. As a pagan, however, Merlin's relationship with Kentigern may not, at least for many years, have been an amicable one. Yet when he sensed he was near the end of his life, he sought out Kentigern and asked to be baptised as a Christian.

Reminders of Merlin are still littered around the area. We drove across a bridge over the River Tweed called Merlington Bridge. A house in the nearby village of Drumelzier is called Merlindale, and the location of his grave is reputed to be close by.

Malc and I really enjoyed looking round the lovely old church at Stobo, with its pele tower and old primitive carved gravestones. It is quiet and peaceful and it was easy to sense that this is indeed an ancient place with its many Dark Age legends. The landscape has changed. Gone is the ancient primeval forest. Gone are the wolves, the bears and the boars. But the echoes are still here. Kentigern's stone which he made into a temporary altar still remains, outside what continues to be known as Altarstone Farm.

We intended to set off to find it, but before doing so we went back into the church to soak up its age and history, much of which is still unclear. In the north aisle, resembling Kentigern's Saxon chapel, is a lovely stained-glass window showing St Kentigern baptising a kneeling Merlin, the wild but wise man of the forest.

We finally left Stobo and followed what we thought was the road to Altarstone Farm, but sadly we just couldn't find it. Even so, it was worth the drive up the tiny road, which took us high up on to the hills, their summits sprinkled with snow, but clear. We looked down on to a huge valley and vista, the valley of the River Tweed. We watched as it flowed along, twisting and turning, its tributaries joining and swelling its waters. It was truly gorgeous.

Malc and I had enjoyed an adventure – a journey into the unknown looking back into history and feeling its atmosphere. This is an ancient land of mystery and legend, continually changing yet also the same, and with many stories to tell if we know where to look and how to listen. Like so many places we have visited on our pilgrimages, the past could have seemed so very far away. What relevance does it have for our lives today? Yet, to me, all of this history, folklore and folk memory does take us back. These were still our people, our land. The echoes and the stories are still there. They are part of who we were, and also who we now are!

Hildas Seal

ST HILDA OF WHITBY

Whitby is a lovely town on the North Yorkshire coast, adjacent to the North York Moors. There is a variety of towns and scenery here, from the busy resorts of Scarborough and Bridlington, clifftops famous for seabirds and small traditional fishing villages with their quaint harbours.

It was a crisp, blustery, early spring day when we arrived, and Whitby seemed to be bursting at the seams. It is something of an understatement to say that Whitby is a popular town. Its popularity is understandable as there are many attractions here. As well as an old harbour still bringing in boats full of crabs and famous Whitby scampi every day, a new marina adjoins the harbour. Yachts are lined up, sail ropes hissing and flapping in the breeze. The town rises up on both sides of the harbour and the River Esk, which flows into the sea here. The towering cliffs and crags of the West and East Cliff almost encircle the harbour entrance. The West Cliff, with its terraces and crescents of Georgian houses, now caters for the many tourists; the East Cliff remains unspoilt, its attraction being Whitby Abbey. This was the focus of our visit, being the site of St Hilda's monastery.

On this east side of the harbour buildings rise up in terraces as they climb the slopes of the cliffs, their characteristic red-tiled roofs prominent against the clear blue sky. The tops of both cliffs are wonderful vantage points to see the wide-ranging vistas below, and the view from the West Cliff shows the dramatic ruins of the abbey standing majestic on the skyline. Traditional warehouses and wharves stand alongside the harbour, once the town's blubber houses and fish markets, evidence of the successful whaling industry. Now gentrified, some of these warehouses are the town's ubiquitous fish-and-chip shops – a famous attraction. Others are upmarket seafood restaurants, some with balconies fronting on to the harbour.

At the industry's height there were fifty-five whaling ships here, comprising a major part of Whitby's economy. Blubber brought here was used for many things. At this time, before the advent of tourists, Whitby can't have been the sweetest-smelling town. The whaling ships may have gone, but they are not forgotten. On the top of West Cliff stands a now much weathered sixteen-foot-tall jaw from a bowhead whale, a reminder of these former and very different times.

From this point you can also see the statue of James Cook, the famous explorer and a Whitby mariner. In the streets below East Cliff behind the harbour is the old town, with its maze of small winding cobbled streets, squashed into a space between the harbour and the cliff. Geared to the tourist trade, there are many lovely shops here.

Whitby is an old atmospheric town which, with a Viking name, dates back to the tenth century. It flourished and yet even with such an ancient history the town we see today is not the earliest established here. At some point the settlement moved down to the harbourside from the abbey headland, where evidence of long habitation from prehistoric times has been found. It was here too on this headland that Hilda's abbey flourished.

The geological history of the area is also important in characterising Whitby, giving another important feature. Millions of years ago this area was submerged under a warm tropical sea. When it became land, fossils were abundant, especially around Whitby, and these are still a major part of Whitby's heritage, with fossil shops found amongst the winding streets of the old town. This heritage is recognised in the town's coat of arms, which includes a picture of three ammonites.

When Bram Stoker wrote his famous Gothic novel *Dracula*,

he set the early part of the story in Whitby, where the Count was shipwrecked and cast ashore. A Goth culture has grown up around this story, and an annual Goth Festival is held here, bringing with it people dressed all in black, matched by black hair and make-up and their own particular type of music.

Quite unexpectedly, this coincides with another Whitby specialism – jet! The town is famed for this rare and unusual stone, which is found along this section of the Yorkshire coast and in very few other places. In its natural state jet is brown in colour and light in weight, looking very much like a splinter of wood, but it is a stone and is sometimes mistaken for coal. Jet is in fact the fossilised remains of the araucaria, which we know by its more familiar name of the monkey puzzle tree. This tree apparently grew in abundance here in the Jurassic period. Shaped, polished and set into a range of jewellery, jet is unusual, striking and beautiful. Walking through the twisting streets of the old town, there is a succession of jet shops.

Its popularity was at its zenith in the mid to late nineteenth century, when after the death of her beloved husband, Albert, Queen Victoria took jet as her only jewel, establishing its role in mourning. Everyone had to follow this trend in order to show empathy for Victoria's bereaved situation. Of course black would not be the automatic choice of everyone else. Most women of wealth and status would have much preferred to wear and show off their extravagant, colourful, expensive jewellery. Jet's saving grace was its lightness; it could be heavily ornamented and be quite flamboyant without discomfort when worn.

Malc and I went into the Whitby Jet Heritage Centre at the very top of the old town. Here is the only remaining example of an almost complete nineteenth-century jet jeweller's workshop, complete with workbenches and tools. Beside this is a modern jewellery shop owned by Hal and his daughter Imogen. I am grateful to Imogen for spending time with me to explain about the history and current work of the industry. Imogen told me that jet had been known of and worked here for many centuries, but its heyday was in the latter part of the nineteenth century, becoming the obligatory fashion of Victoria. Today jet is highly polished, set into gold and silver and often complemented by precious stones and fossils. However, Victorian jet was different. Generally, it was not polished and no refinement or embellishment could be added. Only brooch fasteners and necklace bales were in metal, and this was almost always brass. To compensate, people would include elaborate three-dimensional decoration. This forced popularity made jet one of Whitby's major industries. It was a popular and altogether safer profession than fishing and whaling and was highly esteemed. Apprenticeships were long, from six to nine years, but compensation came in the form of good wages and professional respect. A quirky industry tradition was the giving of brown bowler hats to workers in recognition of their excellence in skill. Old photographs show these workers at their jewellery benches wearing their bowler hats. Ordinary people and customers, on seeing them wearing their prestigious bowler hats, knew that they were in the top echelons of their trade.

"It was very much a male preserve, and still is," said Imogen. "Even today there are only two women jet jewellers in Whitby."

And one of them is Imogen.

I asked about the quantity of jet still being found. She explained that there is still enough for Whitby's needs, but finding it is an art in itself. There are six local experts. The best time to find it, I learned, is after a heavy storm, complete with lashing, crashing waves. This is when the experts go out. The sea brings jet ashore; also, the pounding of the sea against the cliffs breaks off pieces of rock where seams of jet may be found. Deliberately attacking the rocks and cliffs to find jet is illegal, rather different to the nineteenth century, when the cliffs were regularly blasted to release the jet held in the seams of rock. It had been a fascinating insight and I thanked Imogen for her time.

Close by the heritage centre are the famous 199 stone steps, which lead up from the town on to the headland. This is an ancient route trodden for thousands of years by a succession of travellers and pilgrims as well as notable visitors such as kings, queens, bishops, marauding Vikings and no doubt countless others. Climbing this steep promontory, as so many thousands have done before, gives truly awe-inspiring views along the coastline and down to the harbour and town.

At the top the splendour of the site itself opens out to a wide and beautiful vista of coast, cliffs and sea. On the day we visited it was blustery with rough seas, white horses riding in to crash against the cliffs, probably a good jet-seeking day. It was also clear enough to see for miles. The town below is indeed old, but the inhabited area on the top of this headland predates the town, people having lived here since the Stone Age. This headland settlement was called Streanshalch. The origins of the name are still unclear, but 'halc' is thought to mean headland, which makes sense. In the seventh century this settlement was a thriving Anglian village. It was pagan until King Oswiu of Northumbria founded a Christian monastery here. This flourished when Hilda came here as abbess. Today the abbey church stands in ruins, adding to the atmosphere of this evocative spot. The huge cliffs are subject to sea erosion, and the headland would probably have been bigger in Hilda's time than it is now. Nevertheless the area still looks very much as it did when King Oswiu founded his first church here in 670.

Malc and I were staying in a country-house hotel on the outskirts of Whitby, a welcome oasis of calm contrasting with the busy, vibrant tourist centre. Like us, most of the hotel guests were enjoying just a short break. On our first evening sitting in the bar for a pre-dinner drink, a couple close by spoke to us.

"It's a lovely hotel, isn't it?"

And we agreed.

"We are sorry we only booked one night. It was such a good offer we thought we would bring our grandson as a treat."

"It was a great offer," we concurred. "We saw it advertised in a magazine."

"We found it in the *Yorkshire Post*," they countered.

The next morning we fell into conversation with the couple at the next table. The man told us it was his wife's birthday, and they had come to celebrate.

"It's really lovely here, isn't it?" the husband remarked.

We agreed.

"We only came up from Scarborough," he continued, "but we saw it advertised in the *Yorkshire Post*. It was just too good an offer to miss!"

Later in town we recognised another couple from the hotel; they were enjoying a mid-morning tea break. We joined them.

"What do you think of the hotel?" they asked when our pot of tea had arrived.

"We think it's really nice," we replied. "We would definitely come again."

"We only came up from Bridlington," the husband explained, "but it was such a good offer. We saw it advertised in the *Yorkshire Post*!"

On leaving the café and the hotel guests, Malc and I smiled at each other. We realised we had learned two things, and very important ones at that. First, the *Yorkshire Post* is clearly the most important newspaper to read; and secondly, it seems by far the best place to find great offers for short breaks! We filed away both these revelations for possible use another time!

So, suitably refreshed and reliably informed about the above important Yorkshire tradition, we set off up the headland to find Hilda where a much older Yorkshire tradition of pilgrimage to Whitby took place. The abbey ruins here are a landmark clearly visible and imposing in their grandeur. They sit in splendour as they have for hundreds of years. The abbey complex would originally have been much larger, but I'm sure that this church would always have been the focus for travellers. Its dramatic setting cannot fail to make an impact.

I spoke to one of the English Heritage staff who manage this site. I asked her what seemed in retrospect a rather obvious question.

"Why do people come here?" (Duh!)

She told me that over 150,000 people visit the site every year, and it is one of Whitby's most popular attractions.

"There are a number of reasons why they come. Most come, as you would expect, simply because it is part and parcel of coming to Whitby, and people enjoy the expansive views and sea air. Also," she continued, "many visitors are members of English Heritage and they make good use of their membership and make many return visits."

"Would you say any people come purposely for its sense of spirituality and Christian heritage?"

She had to think about that, but then said, "Yes, I think some do, a few."

This was a heartening response, as this was precisely why Malc and I had come.

The abbey ruins people see today are still magnificent. The earliest ruins date from the twelfth century, most in beautiful Gothic style, with elegant details, and soaring Gothic arches point up to heaven. Even on a bright spring day with a clear blue sky it is a wild, blustery place, treeless and windswept, the whole headland still giving the feeling of isolation and remoteness. It begs the question why had it been a successful settlement for over 1,800 years? Why live and build here at all, in such an inaccessible and seemingly forbidding spot? Yet in these early times it would not have seemed so isolated. Roads were few, often dangerous, and most travel would probably have been by sea. So Whitby's headland was more accessible than it seems at first glance. Yes, it was exposed and windswept, but it was also relatively fertile for growing crops and rearing livestock. The discovery of water cisterns, however, seems to suggest there was no natural water source, but this was obviously not an insurmountable problem. This high point gave a sense of security, offering protection from potential enemies, quickly spotted from the elevated viewpoint.

We enjoyed strolling round the lovely ruins. But, whilst most people's interest focused on the abbey, our main focus was on another part of this area altogether, even though it was hidden underground. Here, under the grass and flowers of the wider concourse, unknowingly trampled on by the visitors, lies the first abbey, established by a king and made famous by Hild, later St Hilda.

In these Dark Age times there was a strong link between royalty and the patronage of religious houses. Hilda, born in

617, was herself part of the Northumbrian royal family, related to both King Edwin and King Oswiu. It was not uncommon for women of royal houses to become nuns. Ebba was a daughter of King Oswiu, and she became abbess of Coldingham Priory, higher up the east coast in what is now Scotland.

We know Hilda's abbey was here, but there is no longer a trace of it above ground. Archaeologists have found traces of both stone and wooden buildings, but what these were is still unclear. Indeed, no one is exactly sure where the abbey was located, nor how large it was. Much more is known about Hilda herself. She was devout, but only entered the convent at the age of thirty. She went first to Hartlepool and then transferred to Whitby as abbess, where she remained for the rest of her life. Hilda followed the somewhat idiosyncratic form of Christianity which came to be called Celtic Christianity, but we don't know if this is what they called it themselves.

In the early days of missionaries in Britain seeking Christian converts, it wasn't just one stream of thought which prevailed. It is generally accepted that Augustine, sent by Pope Gregory, came to Southern England, landing in Kent in 597, and from here he set about his mission. When the English King Ethelbert was baptised this paved the way for further Christian conversions, especially in Southern England. Other missionaries succeeded Augustine, Paulinus being one, and he travelled further north, reputedly converting King Edwin of Northumbria in 627. But other Christian influences also held sway, especially in the North and Scotland. Missionaries from Ireland with their own ways were also influential, as evidenced by Columba in Iona. These various influences led to the development of an independent Church based on Celtic tradition. This took hold and survived mostly in a small area of Northern and Eastern England and Scotland. The basic tenets of their faith did not differ from that of Rome, but its organisation and certain practices were different. Main examples seem to be that the monks' tonsure was different from the norm, and also the date of Easter was calculated differently. This became an issue of much greater importance, and would be a pivotal point of argument. Other differences centred on organisation and monastic practice. Women in what we have come to call the Celtic Church were welcomed, revered, and encouraged to take leadership roles.

Whitby under Hilda's leadership became a successful double monastery and abbey, which included both monks and nuns, albeit in separate sections and living quarters. This was not uncommon, and her leadership of both was not considered controversial. Men and women lived in separate, probably individual, cells, most likely built of wood. Life here was not one of great comfort, but neither was it harsh or frugal. The surrounding land was fertile, and as well as providing some of their own food they also traded goods – particularly artefacts produced at the abbey. Finds such as combs, buckles and book covers have been found, and these items were made with great skill and many refinements.

Hilda also ran a school here, for both boys and girls, and her results speak for themselves for we know that at least five of her students went on to become bishops. This includes St Wilfrid, who unfortunately forsook his loyalty to his abbess in favour of advancement in the Church.

By all accounts Hilda was a remarkable woman, and the success of her abbey was reputed to be due solely to her character, her intelligence, her wisdom and her personal expression of faith. She was greatly admired and respected, and it was Hilda herself who was the focus of pilgrimage at Whitby during her lifetime as an abbess.

But what was it about her which made her so special, for special she was? Visitors (pilgrims) came in large numbers to see her, sometimes many times. Some came in times of stress, worry or sickness, some for prayer and forgiveness, but most came simply to see Hilda herself, most often to seek counsel and advice. We mostly think of pilgrims who travelled to shrines and to physical relics to absorb the spirit and strength of the saint for healing and forgiveness. This was not always so. The early Church was concerned with evangelism, spreading Christian knowledge of Jesus and the Gospels, and developing the Church. There were no relics at

Hilda's abbey. What there was was Hilda herself. Her faith, encouragement and wisdom were the qualities which drew people, and pilgrimage allowed them to meet and learn from her. Within her abbey she ensured that all the monks and nuns were educated in reading and writing. Paramount was ensuring an understanding of the Gospels. She encouraged prayer and meditation, but also debate and some freethinking in a church that was relatively free from dogma. Each Celtic church and abbey had some freedom to develop in its own way. Churches were only loosely aligned, with a relatively flat structure, free from a bureaucratic hierarchy. Nor were the pilgrims here just ordinary people. Hilda's counsel was sought by kings, queens and bishops, and on more than one occasion her highly valued opinions and advice, as well as spiritual guidance, were rewarded by a monetary gift to the abbey. It prospered and grew, and people came here for tutelage to gain admission to the Church.

Times were changing, however, and in the late seventh century the Celtic Church, independent and isolated from mainstream Roman Christianity, faced a crisis. There were those who wanted to bring the Church into the fold of Rome, one of whom was Wilfred, despite his long association with Whitby. Equally, many others wanted to continue with their own idiosyncratic spiritual and ascetic form of worship. But there was disharmony too in the fact of the difference in the date of Easter, which was not the same as that of Rome. This proved to be the perfect excuse Wilfred needed to force a confrontation. As a result he convinced King Oswiu to convene a conference of the main leaders of the church in 677. This became known as the famous Synod of Whitby, and this venue was a testament to the high esteem which Hilda commanded. The synod's purpose was to consider whether the Celtic Church should submit to the authority of the Pope. In the end the pro-Roman faction, led by Wilfred, won the day. He convinced the king that the Roman way was the one true way. The Celtic Church with its own ways had been given its death knell, and all existing churches and religious houses were now forced to turn their faces to Rome.

This did not happen quickly, however. Wilfrid was greatly rewarded with bishoprics, land and money, but he was not well liked. Nevertheless, Hilda's abbey continued to flourish until the time of the Viking incursions in the eighth century, when the headland and abbey were abandoned.

Hilda became ill at the age of sixty, but lived another few years, dying in 680.

It was many years before people returned, but in the 1100s the abbey was rebuilt, becoming rich on the reputation of Hilda. The ruins of this abbey church still testify with its exposed grandeur to its former glory days. Its stones still speak of power and wealth, its soaring walls reaching up to heaven. Hilda's wish had been to simply build and run a house of prayer and devotion to God, and the site still resounds to Hilda's influence. She was a woman who commanded the respect of kings, a charismatic woman, and an inspiring place it still is. Despite the many people visiting, like us, their voices are carried away by the soughing of the wind, and it feels a very peaceful spot, the echoes of the past carrying in the wind. Hilda's message still resounds. She was a woman who influenced life in what we call the Dark Ages, but were they dark? Not with people like Hilda, who were rather beacons of light.

The next morning we were heading home. Our breakfast friends from the next table were leaving too. As we were loading our luggage, they got into a brand-new bright-red Morgan. Now in his sixties, the man told us he had owned Morgans all his adult life. He ordered his first, he told us, at the age of eighteen years, and had to wait five years before it arrived! Times change. Morgan is now the only car company owned by and still built in Britain. The waiting time for a new one is now only a few months. It may be the only remaining British-made and -owned car, but it is still one to be proud of. As he got into the driving seat we looked at the sumptuous black leather with distinctive red piping. It certainly was a lovely car. With the hood down they raced off with a roar into the Yorkshire countryside.

I wasn't quite ready for home, and Malc and I drove back

into Whitby. I decided I couldn't go home without some jet, even if the jewellery is rather expensive. In the end I managed to buy two pieces, antique and unpolished with a simple cross raised, carved out of the stone. I thought one would be perfect as a birthday present for my mum; with mine there is no chain or bale, but I really like it.

I later took it to a local jewellery repair shop in Carlisle. The jeweller added a bale for me, so it now has a chain too. It is decidedly wearable and a lovely souvenir of our enjoyable visit to Whitby.

These are photographs of Whitby Abbey.

ST WILFRID AND THE BATTLE FOR CELTIC CHRISTIANITY: ST WILFRID AT HEXHAM

Hexham is a little gem of a town, situated on a bluff high above the River Tyne. This is Hadrian's Wall country in Northumberland, and Hexham is a popular stopping-off point for visitors to the forts spaced out along the wall. A well-deserved World Heritage Site, Hadrian's Wall stretches across the narrow divide west beyond Carlisle to Newcastle at Wallsend. As a barrier to keep the barbarians in Scotland, the wall certainly stood the test of time. The Romans knew how to build. In an area still essentially unspoilt, the forts and 'mile castles' give a fascinating insight into Roman life in this very remote outpost of the empire. These Roman marvels blend unobtrusively into the landscape, one of great natural beauty.

Most people, though not all, probably come to Hexham by way of their interest in the Romans and realise what a lovely place it is. My purpose though is different, for I have come to find another unique treasure, located in the abbey, albeit from a few centuries later.

From the car park below the bluff, steep lanes take you up into the town, where a mixture of period houses hints at its history. The medieval layout of the town is clearly visible in today's Hexham. Narrow streets and twisty lanes and closes radiate out from a small central open area and marketplace. Dominating this area is Hexham Abbey, the focus for my visit. It is a formidable structure in a small space, old, majestic and towering over the central part of the town.

Heading for the entrance, Malc was approached by a disabled man in his wheelchair.

"I wonder if you could help me?" he asked.

Malc asked how he could help.

"Could you assist me out of my chair and into my car, and then put my chair into the boot?"

A specially adapted car stood by the kerb, and Malc started to push the chair round to the driver's door.

"Before I get in," he said, "let me show you the car and all its clever adaptations."

Clearly, he was proud of it, and Malc, an avid car enthusiast, was keen to look, and he was impressed. The man also told us he was a volunteer guide at the abbey, and he was on his way home at the end of his shift. He spoke lovingly and authoritatively about the abbey and we felt we had been introduced to its history and charm before we even stepped inside.

"Enjoy your visit," he said, and we waved like old friends as he finally drove away.

Like many popular tourist attractions, Hexham Abbey has adapted to the modern world and the modern visitor. There are glassed-in displays and interactive devices along with the ubiquitous café. Yet to me it is still the walls and interior of the abbey which speak most clearly. I have been to countless churches and cathedrals, and yet I found myself really loving Hexham Abbey. My reasons even to myself were unclear, but there was something about the atmosphere and character. The fact of it having changed and developed over the centuries seemed to make it alive. To me, Roman remnants and everything in between, till now, seem to create a harmonious whole, representing as it does the whole range of Hexham history. 'Hogback' grave covers along with Saxon grave covers stand alongside Roman memorials and medieval knights' graves. A tiny copper Communion cup 1,000 years old, slightly bashed, but beautiful, vies for attention with features that no longer exist anywhere else, the twelfth-century monks' stairs being a prime example. These impressive yet worn and eroded sandstone stairs descend into the church crossing from what was originally the monks' dormitory. This entrance opened

Sculptures in Hexham Abbey.

The twelfth-century monks' stairs in Hexham Abbey – the only ones remaining in the UK.

directly into the church and meant the monks did not need to venture outside when attending night-time masses. They were no doubt extremely grateful in dark, cold, wet weather. It wasn't hard to imagine the thousands of monks who had used the stairs over the centuries, their presence echoing down through to the present.

But I digress. The real purpose of my visit was to see an even older and original part of the abbey. Only rediscovered during some restoration work in the eighteenth century, below the current nave is the crypt of what was the church of St Wilfrid. Dating from the seventh century, there is little else like it anywhere in the UK.

Educated in Whitby under the tutelage of Hilda and in the tradition of northern Celtic/Saxon Christianity, nevertheless Wilfrid turned from this to believe in the overarching and valid power of the Roman Catholic Church. He travelled several times to Rome and visited Popes there. Yet at home he was not a popular man.

At the famous Synod of Whitby, Wilfrid spoke forcefully about his belief in the Roman Church and convinced King Oswiu of Northumbria that the Celtic Church should conform to Roman rule.

Wilfrid's vehemence won the day and the idiosyncratic Celtic doctrine, based on prayer, deep spirituality and learning, was in crisis, and the decision of the synod spelled the death knell for it. Wilfrid was rewarded for his efforts, the Pope awarding him the bishopric of York. Further power enhanced his position when Queen Ethelreda of Northumbria gifted him huge tracts of land centred on Hexham. Despite this, he was not liked in his home county and parts of the Church distanced themselves from him, blaming him for the Celtic Church's loss of power to Rome. But he had great influence and he built a church here in Hexham. The church, of which only the crypt remains, possibly unique because of its age, and also the fact that it was built of stone was highly unusual at the time.

It is hard to forget the Romans here, and it is their legacy which gave Wilfrid his resource: stones recycled from the miles of wall and forts. It is this continuity which is impressive at Hexham.

Additionally, it is believed Wilfrid used stone from Corbridge, further east from Hexham. A history of stonemasonry probably also explains his ability to build his stone chapel. Somewhere in the area there may still have been stoneworkers who had retained their skills down the centuries after the Romans left. This beautiful crypt remains a testament to the durability of existing stones and the strength and accuracy of the building blocks. Apart from three recent additional steps, the whole crypt remains exactly as it was built in the seventh century – a remarkable survivor.

Originally above the crypt in what is now the nave of the abbey was the upper church, with the crypt having a special purpose of its own, part of its space being designated a shrine where pilgrims would come in their thousands to pray to the venerated saint and to ask for healing and forgiveness.

The question is, though, if Wilfrid was unpopular, why did pilgrims come to Hexham? Certainly they came to the shrine, but whose shrine? No one knows for sure, but it's almost certain that there were actual relics here, thought to have been relics of St Andrew and brought here by Wilfrid. Andrew was such an important saint, and Wilfrid would have known the extra kudos such relics would give him. These relics were said to lie in honour in the shrine. Whether people really believed them to be of St Andrew isn't known, but they were considered to be of great age and immense sanctity, worthy of pilgrimage as real holy relics. For relics of such purported venerability, people would have travelled great distances. When the relics disappeared no one knows, and they are now a mystery, yet the chapel where they were displayed is still here in this remarkable remnant from Saxon times.

The entrance to the crypt is via a set of steep steps from the nave. The top three are recent additions necessary because the floor of the nave is now higher. The walls at the sides are built of large sandstone slabs and it is obvious that they have been reused. Such stones are evident throughout. At the bottom of the stairs it is like entering a cave. A small vestibule area leads into a small barrel-vaulted room where the shrine would have been. To each side of this room are small corridors, both now sealed off, but which originally would have led outside. One corridor provided access for pilgrims, the other for monks. There are sconces for candles, but even today it is still dark and cold, and there are no windows. At certain times there must have been a steady stream of visitors, one way in and one way out, with the shrine in the middle. The exit was up the steps (the way I had come down) and on into the church.

It is all so small and must have seemed extremely claustrophobic then, with so many pilgrims pressing in, wanting to see. Impatient, dusty from their travels, many were probably unclean and smelly, and the area would have been noisy with people conversing excitedly about what they were likely to see. It may seem an odd thing for us today, but in the Dark and Middle Ages pilgrimage was immensely popular, providing exciting journeys, but also for an extremely religious nation it meant a great deal and was also a way to expurgate sins and seek healing for there was no conventional cure for so many kinds of disease.

The crypt provided a wonderful slice of a time in history when so much is still unclear. I was so glad to have seen it. Stones *can* speak, and these stones, many beautifully decorated and with marks and engravings, told of how pagan Romans in the area may have lived and how their homes were recycled into a different kind of building – a church of Christian faith.

I was sad to leave. Malc and I set off back through the town down the hilly streets. Previously I had noticed another ancient landmark – Hexham Old Jail – and I thought I'd like to have a look. A tall, square building of golden sandstone, it dates from 1330. It is the oldest remaining jail in Britain and was purpose-built.

It isn't how you expect a prison to look or operate. There are no individual cells, but rather three floors. On the first floor well-off prisoners would live; the ground floor was for those less well off. However, prisoners had to pay to be kept in prison; otherwise there was no food, heating or clothes. Those who could not pay were thrown into the lower dungeon, without light, heat or food.

There was a great opportunity to show how the prison would have looked and operated as a prison, but they have not done this. I was very disappointed. The upper floor, where the jailer lived, could have been laid out as he would have lived in it, but the room was empty except for a small display about the Border reivers. A real missed opportunity! Never mind – I had seen some amazing things in the day, so I could take one disappointment!

This area is saturated with history, and even today it isn't hard to imagine those hardy pilgrims finding their way across cold, often wet and inhospitable country of hills, moorland, bogs and rivers – a land also studded with the remains of an even earlier people echoing in the forts along the ancient Roman wall. Go to Hexham, but not *just* for the Romans.

I will walk secure and blessed
In every clime and coast
In name of God the father
And Son and Holy Ghost

St Columba

ST COLUMBA'S HEBRIDEAN HOME: IONA

The little island of Iona has been a special place for hundreds of years and is as popular today. Columba, often remembered as the father of Scottish Christianity, made his home here, and his reputation has not diminished over time. Malc and I found ourselves as day visitors here as we were staying on the island of Mull instead. Mull massively overshadows tiny Iona, being a large, beautiful island. With its prevalence of wildlife, from otters to sea eagles, it has become an extremely popular place for nature lovers, so much so that to us Mull seemed in many ways to be a victim of its own success. The very things people come to see, golden eagles, deer and dolphins bring people in their droves, meant a feeling of impending saturation to us. Admittedly, it was August, so yes, it was a very busy time, but the narrow roads in the more popular places were almost uncomfortably busy. Understandably, everyone was desperate to see wildlife, and we noticed groups of people all over the island, in laybys and on beaches and verges, anxiously hoping to see something. And yes, you can see things, as we did, for example, a sea eagle perching nonchalantly in a tree. But it seemed that the whole reason for people's visits has meant it is in danger of spoiling its very quality and reputation for peace, beauty, wildness and anticipation. Getting away from crowds, traffic and noise is increasingly hard to do.

Before driving across Mull to Iona, we visited another tiny island only a few hundred yards off Mull's coast. This island is Ulva. Most people will have heard of the Highland clearances, which mostly took place in the nineteenth century. These remain dark days for the Scots, days when farmers and crofters, some of whom had been resident for generations in the same place, were forcibly evicted by the landowners. They wanted to use their land for sheep farming or some other lucrative trade and this meant their tenants were considered uneconomical and a nuisance. By claiming back their land, these tenants were cruelly evicted without compensation or without being given alternative homes or livelihood. This tiny island of Ulva provides a perfect cameo of these clearances, reflecting in miniature what happened on a massive scale throughout the Highlands – not just in Argyle, where Ulva and Mull are found.

A small motorised dinghy takes across anyone who wants to visit Ulva, taking literally minutes to get there. There doesn't seem much to attract visitors, but there is a popular pub here, with customers sitting happily in an outside space, enjoying the weather and of course food and drink. No doubt they also like to watch the comings and goings of the ferry directly in front. This lovely spot, quiet and relaxed, belies its status in the nineteenth century. For 600 years it had been the hub and residence of the McQuarrie clan. Unfortunately, the clan chief was forced to sell the island to pay debts, and in 1830 it was bought by a Mr Francis Clarke. He immediately set about transforming the island according to his own interests, which meant the eviction of the island tenants. In 1837 there was a population of 604 predominantly self-supporting and self-sufficient small farmers and crofters. By 1881 only fifty-seven people were left. Clarke's reputation for cruelty and inhuman practices was one of the worst of all the landowners. No one was allowed to complain of the eviction and treatment. Anyone who did so would immediately have their roof thatch torched, their houses burned down in front of them, and with all their belongings still inside. We learned that the corner of the island by the pub and ferry was called Desolation Point, this being where the now homeless and jobless families huddled together, wondering what they were going to do.

So we set off for Iona, with a long drive across what is called the Ross of Mull, Ross meaning an isolated peninsula. Certainly there are few settlements along the way. Before we arrived at the ferry to the island we came to a village called Bunessan about six miles from Iona. Only a few hundred people live here, but nevertheless it is a busy centre serving many more small and isolated communities. This is a coastal village on the sea loch Lathaich.

Now, anyone coming into contact with young children over the last few years can't fail to have heard or seen the children's programme *Balamory*, based at a preschool at Balamory. This in real names is Mull's capital, Tobermory. Once having been there and then seen the programme, it is hard not to spot some familiar landmarks. The regular characters too have memorable names. In Bunessan we spotted a *Balamory* favourite sitting quietly in the village car park, indeed it was hard not to see it, for it was Edie McCredie's bright-yellow bus.

There was another meaningful thing too about Bunessan, which was a pilgrimage coincidence. When Malc and I were in Norwich, impressed by St Julian's Cell*, we also heard that changes were happening. The community of All Hallows had been involved in running the Julian Centre and guest house for many years. The numbers involved from All Hallows diminished over time until in 2017 only four of the nuns remained and the Church felt that the community was no longer sustainable; the four remaining sisters were having to disperse. We heard that one sister, Pamela, whom we had met in Norwich had decided that when she left she would relocate to Scotland, knowing that she had been called to go to Bunessan, where she hoped to establish a new ministry.

Six miles further on, we waited to board the ferry to Iona. When we left it was at full capacity, and soon afterwards a passenger shouted that there were dolphins alongside the boat. En masse people rushed to the side, hoping to see them – so much so that Malc and I thought that the boat was about to tip over and sink!

It seemed like thousands disembarked, everyone heading the same way, away from the small community by the ferry and up to the right, the road to the abbey. Iona, lying off the southern tip of Mull and only three miles by one and a half, seems to be physically

* See chapter on Julian of Norwich, page 201.

overwhelmed by Mull's large land mass, with only around 100 souls living here. Yet despite its small size it vies very well with its larger neighbour, having its very own individual reputation and history. There are some lovely beaches, a hotel and a small village, but it is the heritage of St Columba which is the main attraction here.

Iona is 'Columba's Isle', and he is very much remembered as a Christian missionary, with Iona considered the cradle of Celtic Christianity, which prevailed in Scotland and Northern England until the eighth century. And yet Columba was neither Scottish nor a missionary! In fact he was Irish and had been a priest there. A personal scandal saw Columba leave Ireland as a self-imposed exile, knowing it was very unlikely he would ever return to his native land. So it was in AD 563 that he arrived in Iona with twelve followers, and he felt immediately homesick. Intending to stay, however, he located his settlement at a point on the island where he could not see Ireland. So, homesick or not, this became his home, and even though he had not come as a missionary he grew in faith, wisdom and character, becoming a religious leader with great influence, which brought people to see him. Nor was his influence restricted to Scotland; it was also felt across England in Northumberland where he sent his follower Aidan to help King Oswald in their efforts to convert his people.

An abbey developed on Iona, and it became a place of reverence to Columba and a place of pilgrimage. Indeed, a specific pilgrim trail can still be discerned, which went from Grass Point on the east coast of Mull following waymarkers, crosses and standing stones across the inhospitable land to Iona. These stones continued on the island leading up to the abbey, often used as praying stones before the journey's end. Some of these stones and crosses still stand; others, many broken, are in the local museum.

Today the abbey is still beautiful, its surroundings unspoilt and uplifting. People say that Iona is special in many ways, that in fact the whole island is a shrine, not just to Columba but to God himself. In a metaphysical and almost supernatural way, it is also claimed there are special places where the air is 'thin'. Iona is reputed to be one of these places, where the material physical world and the spiritual world are very close, and it is possible to have a great sense of being close to God. Yet Iona Abbey and other associated buildings faced destruction, like so many others, in Scotland as a result of the Scottish Reformation, so we can't blame Henry VIII this time. But the difference is that this abbey was restored and thrives today as a church for regular worship, for pilgrims and visitors. The saviour of Columba's abbey was the Reverend George MacLeod, who felt inspired and guided to restore it and oversee the work, in 1938. In 1899, the 8th Duke of Argyle, who owned the island (and his family still does), gave the monastic buildings to the Church of Scotland for safekeeping. (Therein lies the irony in that it was the Church of Scotland which ruined it in the first place!) It was the Reverend MacLeod who really made the difference, and it is to him we owe today's restoration and spiritually flourishing abbey with its many volunteers who continue to maintain the spiritual focus of St Columba. Today it is a partnership with Historic Environment Scotland, who maintain the fabric whilst the Iona Community promotes worship, spiritual development and the essence of Columba.

Much of the island surrounding the monastic and abbey buildings is very open and windswept, with nowhere being far from the island's beaches. There is clear, refreshing air here in the sense that it is not so very different from when Columba was here. Although he spent the rest of his life on Iona, we know that he did travel and we know of his missionary journeys. It's believed he converted the King of the Picts to Christianity, and this would have entailed difficult travel to the east of Scotland. Legend tells us that he travelled to what is modern Inverness and passed Loch Ness and crossed the River Ness. Here, as he waited to cross, he saw a ferocious and dangerous beast in the water and was told by locals that the monster had killed people. This was in August AD 565, and was the first recorded sighting of Nessie, the Loch Ness monster. The incident was reported by Adnam after Columba's death when he was writing the biography of the saint.

Despite the seemingly large crowd which came over on the ferry, everywhere seemed quiet. In the abbey church, and on walking around, we wondered where everyone was. They headed up towards the abbey, but when we got there they all seemed to have disappeared. We headed back and what had been a somewhat dull day suddenly became a very rainy one. We dashed into the hotel to escape the deluge and realised where everyone seemed to be. It was crowded – a fug of wet clothes and boots was all-pervading and the noise was raucous. The windows had misted up and we just managed to find a seat. Like us, everyone was sheltering, laughing, eating, drinking, keeping out of the rain before heading to the ferry. The atmosphere was relaxed, and despite the rain it was a lovely end to our day. The malt whisky we drank was warming.

I took out a small packet which was in my bag. In the abbey shop I had bought some earrings made from the rare Iona gemstone, a kind of marble/agate found only here and in a few places on Mull. Local people, knowing where and what to look for, find it often washed up on the beaches, and it is then fashioned and polished into jewellery. I put them on, they looked great. I was pleased with my souvenir. We were so relaxed we almost missed the ferry, and only made it because the man at the barrier saw us running and waited for us. We collected our car at Fionnphort, no more than a cluster of houses, and set off back to our accommodation near Tobermory.

When we again reached Bunessan I remembered the conversation I had managed to have with Sister Pamela, whom I spoke to after she had left Norfolk.

She said, "I spent nineteen years in Norwich working at the Julian House, looking after visitors, giving talks and running retreats. Visitors came from all over the world. It was my community of All Hallows which had been responsible for the restoration of St Julian's Cell, which had been bombed during the Second World War. There were no plans to rebuild it and the leader of our community said St Julian's Cell was too important and her church should not be wiped out. 'Well, you find the money to restore it, then,' she was told, and they did. The Church of St Julian would not be there today were it not for the foresight of All Hallows."

When Sister Pamela realised the community was to disperse

there were only four nuns left. There had been forty-six when she joined. I tried to think how I would feel if I had been in such a situation, having to leave a place I loved and respected, and also facing separation from the sisters I had lived with for so long. I think I would feel stunned, uncertain, and perhaps a little frightened at what lay ahead. But this is me speaking and not Sister Pamela. From her I had no sense of fear or even apprehension. I believe she knew where God wanted her to be, even though it proved to be hundreds of miles from the flat but mellow land of Norfolk to wild, remote, cold and mountainous Scotland. This was what she felt she should do and did.

She continued: "I felt myself continually singing the hymn 'Morning Has Broken', but not knowing why. I then realised that this is sung to the tune called 'Bunessan' and is also the tune for Julian's hymn. This was a message. I looked up 'Bunessan' on the Net and at the same time a cottage for rent flashed up. I made my decision and the cottage was still for rent and I knew that this was what God wanted. I moved into the cottage and began my new life on Mull. Everything just fell into place," she said. "I came with an open mind to be available wherever I was needed, and my ministry is still growing and taking shape. I work ecumenically and have links with local churches and Iona, who all work together, and I preach there too and give talks." She concluded by saying, "Iona is a special place."

But I imagine that even in Columba's time, for those developing faith and learning to live together with many different people, life was not easy. It must be the same today, I thought. I am really glad I have spoken with Sister Pamela. In a short time I found her inspirational and courageous. I know that her ministry will be nothing other than successful and life-changing, both for her and for people she meets.

Cuddly Ducks

ST CUTHBERT AT LINDISFARNE

It seemed like a little adventure as we drove over the tidal causeway to the island, knowing that in a few hours where we were driving would be sea. Surrounded by miles of sand, mudflats and sand dunes, we travelled two miles, often splashing through seawater left stranded after the tide receded. Halfway along, we noticed a wooden hut on a high pole accessed by an external ladder at the side of the causeway. This was a refuge. We, like most visitors, had checked the tide tables and knew when it was safe to cross. Yet some people risk the crossing at the very last minute and find themselves caught by the incoming tide. Climbing the ladder to the refuge keeps them safe, but it is a long wait until the tide turns, or rescuers arrive. In the meantime, they see their car floating away on the waves. It pays to be sensible.

Lindisfarne, also called Holy Island, is small, only three miles by one and a half. It is predominantly low-lying, comprising many sand dunes, few trees and rough pasture, and is often windblown, with one small village at the opposite end from the causeway. But it is also a haven for wildlife, especially seabirds and wild flowers. Whilst walking around we saw lots of wild wallflowers situated, as their name suggests, in walls and rock crevices.

Malc and I were staying on the island, but the vast majority of people come as day visitors. And come they do! Lindisfarne is a magnet for them, and hordes travel across the causeway every day. We spoke to a local shopkeeper, who told us that an average of 3,000 cars arrive every day! In total over 500,000 people visit each year. The small island must certainly seem swamped some of the time. Why so many people? I suppose that it is an adventure to travel, like us, to a place which is an island twice a day. Also there are some lovely walks and beaches, a castle and an abbey, and a pleasant village with the usual shops and cafés. At its heart, however, is the story of how Lindisfarne became the cradle of Christianity in much of Central and Northern England and Lowland Scotland.

Its story begins in what we today call the Dark Ages, with a king called Oswald in the sixth and seventh centuries.

Lindisfarne is an island on the east coast of England in Northumberland in a more northerly part of the county, heading towards Berwick-upon-Tweed. Today it is the most rural county in England, with few large towns or large urban areas. It is also well known for its beauty, especially its coast with its wide sandy beaches and unspoilt fishing villages and castles, some majestic, others ruined, remote and atmospheric.

Being on the east coast, it can also be blustery and stormy, and it is in this area where we read the story of Grace Darling, the daughter of a lighthouse man who braved a terrible storm to rescue sailors in nothing but a rowing boat. In Oswald's time Northumberland was the largest kingdom in Britain. It was truly vast, stretching in a swathe across England from the Humber Estuary, near Hull, across to and including Cumberland and up into much of Lowland Scotland. Its very name signifies its greatness, meaning the land north of the Humber.

Oswald was clearly a powerful and wealthy man, but he was also a great and intelligent warrior and ruler at a time when Britain was in constant turmoil and battle-ready. The other side of this great warrior king, however, was a kind and deeply religious man. His path to kingship had not been an easy one. He had spent most of his early life on Iona; and there, under Columba's influence, he became a devout Christian. But Northumberland, when he came to claim his throne, was a land almost wholly pagan. With great determination, he set about the conversion of his kingdom; an enormous task. Even after a faltering start he was undeterred, asking Iona for help. Columba responded to his call with a volunteer priest, Aidan, who spent the rest of his life working alongside Oswald with a missionary zeal in a land far from easy to convert.

Time and patience paid off. Christianity took hold and grew. Oswald offered Aidan land where he could base himself and establish a centre of Christian faith. Of all the land available Aidan chose the island of Lindisfarne; not a great mystery when looking at Celtic Christianity with its strong emphasis on meditation and solitary living. Both Oswald and Aidan were later made saints, and a statue of Aidan stands proud in the abbey grounds.

Yet, despite their massive influence and dedication, it is, strangely, not these two saints who are most regarded and remembered on Lindisfarne. That honour goes to the greatly venerated Cuthbert, and for many people, then and even now, Cuthbert *is* Lindisfarne. He was greatly loved in his lifetime and famously venerated after his death.

Cuthbert was a Lowland Scot who had spent many years at Melrose Abbey on the banks of the River Tweed, where he became abbot. Almost against his will, he was persuaded to come and live at Lindisfarne. His leadership was legendary, and here he spent the rest of his life.

Just offshore from Holy Island is another tiny island, no more than a stretch of grassy mounds, only 200 yards or so long, and it has become known as Cuthbert's Isle. This is a tidal island too, and at low tide it is possible to walk to it along the rocky beach. On our first morning this was our intention. However, although the main causeway had cleared, Cuthbert's Isle had not. We waited on the beach until it was passable. Whilst waiting, we joined a group of birdwatchers with their great spotting scopes, scanning the sea and rocks around. I asked one of the women if the group was together.

"Yes," she said. "We are a birding group and have come here for the day from Skipton in Yorkshire."

"And have you come to see something in particular?" I queried.

"No, not really, but we have just spotted a pair of red-breasted mergansers."

Now, even I know that this is a relatively uncommon bird. I'm not an RSPB member for nothing! So they had found something unexpected.

"Would you like to see?" she asked me as she started to adjust her scope to my level.

I could see them very clearly, splashing around at the edge of Cuthbert's Isle. I have to confess to not having seen one of these birds before, and it isn't the bird most people associate the island with. The Farne Islands, a few miles up the coast, are famous for birds and also seals and dolphins. From Seahouses, the nearest Northumberland gets to a resort, with its harbour and fish-and-chip shops, sightseeing boat trips take visitors out to the islands every day, weather permitting. There is a huge variety of birds, many visitors remembering the terns, which can be vicious when nesting, swooping down and attacking heads, sometimes even drawing blood. But there is one bird that most people long to see: the puffin. This small, dumpy bird, comical with its colourful beak, thrives here where its diet of sand eels is plentiful. Around 49,000 pairs are resident in these islands, and no doubt most people who see them even in rough seas think the journey worthwhile. As for me, I was looking out for a different bird, the eider duck. These are large birds, up to twenty-four inches, and spend most of their time on the sea. The males in their black-and-white plumage are striking and beautiful and they are a common sight along the Northumberland coast. These were Cuthbert's favourite, possibly because around his tiny island there were many of them, as we saw whilst waiting on the beach to cross over. His love of them caused people to call them 'cuddy ducks', which they still are today.

Then, when the islet was fully uncovered, we began our walk across, a short walk along the beach between rocks and rock pools and huge swathes of seaweed. It was slippery in places, but we stepped on to dry land without overly wet feet. There is little to see: some rough grass, a tiny beach, a small crag with a convenient spot for sitting and Cuthbert's ruined chapel and hermitage. A feature of the Celtic Church was the importance of quiet seclusion and meditation. Many monks, like Cuthbert, felt the need to completely remove themselves to remote places to be alone, often for weeks at a time. It was easy to envision him here, where not many people walked over to this isle. It was peaceful, but windswept, noisy with seabirds and seals bobbing up and down out in the bay, and I could imagine him there.

Later in life he became almost reclusive, moving to an even more remote place, an island called Inner Farne. Here he built another chapel and hermitage. Legend tells us that he built the wall so high that all you could see was sky, so that there were no distractions when he needed to meditate. We seem to have very much lost the tradition of finding places of peace, quiet and tranquillity to enjoy the value of silence, to give rest and rejuvenation to our souls, not just to commune with God, but to commune with ourselves, our inner spirit, away from the seemingly permanent noise of our lives and the world today.

We stayed a while on Cuthbert's Isle, watching the seals in the bay and feeling the freshness of the breeze on our faces. When we clambered over the rock-strewn beach back to the main island we felt refreshed and uplifted. The weather throughout our stay was lovely and sunny, but blustery. On our journey to Holy Island too the weather had been fine. Although living in the Scottish borderlands and we were travelling to England, our journey took us further north since much of Northumberland is parallel to and indeed higher up than some parts of Lowland Scotland. We travelled there just on A-roads, which were really quiet, noticing that the sloping verges were covered in primroses. The hillsides were bright with gorse and thousands of lambs crowded the fields.

The main advantage to us of actually staying on Lindisfarne was that in the mornings, before the causeway was open, and then later, when people had to make their way back across, the island was relatively empty and felt almost like another place altogether. It seemed as if the island calmed down, back to how it would have been years ago, before the advent of tourism. We found that island life was dominated by the tides, quite understandably. Today's economy is dependent on tourists and each shop displayed a different notice daily, saying what times they would open and close depending on the times of the tides, which vary considerably. Some didn't open some days until 11 or 11.30 a.m. and it was strange that as the tide went out there was a real sense of the island slowly filling up. We used some of our quiet time to visit the church.

Built at a much later date than the abbey, it does have Saxon origins. Just inside stands a striking memorable sculpture showing Cuthbert's coffin being carried by pall-bearing monks, a very evocative impression of the time, showing a rough wooden coffin and the monks' garments, lifelike and detailed.

Whilst there, we decided to attend evensong. Sadly, considering the number of people on the island, attendance was sparse; in fact, only six of us. When an elderly retired minister arrived and began the service we found the liturgy different to our usual one at Carlisle Cathedral, but we tried to take part enthusiastically. I was dismayed when she stopped the service and quite pointedly made it clear I had been reciting it wrongly. It must have annoyed her. I felt embarrassed and giggly at the same time. She then told me how to say it.

"OK, let's start again," she said somewhat crossly. "Let's see if we can get it right this time!"

What a welcome! I felt like I was back at school, being told off by my teacher. Malc and I looked at each other, not quite believing what had just happened. Sitting on my left was a young man, who we found out was also a visitor.

He looked at me, smiled and said, "Oh dear," somewhat bemused.

We chatted to him later; he couldn't believe it either. Malc and I wondered if this was why there were only six of us brave enough to risk her wrath!

Despite its popularity, the island is not overly commercialised, but there was one lovely gift shop specialising in the Celtic heritage, and Cuthbert in particular. I was attracted to a necklace with a shell pendant. In the past, particularly in the early Middle Ages, pilgrims would often travel to more than one pilgrimage site, each with a distinct character. A tradition developed whereby each shrine would produce pilgrim badges, often unique to that particular shrine. Pilgrims were excited to buy their badge and have their journey authenticated. Thus began the souvenir, although it was more than simply a reminder of your visit. There was also a ubiquitous badge symbol: a scallop or cockleshell.

These badges were bought in their thousands, and medieval pictures show pilgrims with these badges proudly displayed. Pilgrims would take them home with pride to show their families. There were additional values to the pilgrim badge too. Pilgrims were respected and honoured, and showing off the badges on their journey was literally a 'badge of honour'. At a practical level, this honour had benefits. If in need of food, accommodation or help, simply showing their badge would often result in free hospitality. On a more spiritual level, there was a belief too that the badge was endowed with the spirit and power of the saint it represented, and the pilgrim could tap into this power for healing, forgiveness or whatever else they needed. These badges gave pilgrims confidence, hospitality, respect and a feeling of safety – all things which would sustain them on their journey. I bought the necklace, and this is now my pilgrim badge.

We had intended going off the island to see a little more of the coast, but in the end we never did. We passed our time happily pottering about, visiting the abbey and museum and strolling in the sunshine. Although the island is mostly flat, there is a steep path which leads up to the castle and also the Hough – the highest point, but still only a few hundred feet. We walked up to the Hough via the harbour with its famous old upturned boats, originally used for storage or even little summer houses, some now sadly in a dilapidated state. It was a sunny but windy climb, but when we arrived we were pleased to see that inside a tall stone tower there was a viewing platform pleasantly glassed in, and giving a 360-degree view. When the tide is in, you can see Lindisfarne as an island, but other sights are impressive too. Bamburgh Castle is close by, sitting atop a huge crag, rebuilt now, but originally the base for King Oswald, its site spectacular and giving warnings about possible invaders, especially the Vikings. It was a true stronghold and a symbol of Oswald's great power. The Farne Islands too were visible a little further away, and Inner Farne could be seen clearly, still showing the chapel and hermitage where Cuthbert spent the last years of his life.

There was an easier way down from the Hough, but we again took the longer path, following the rough footpath across ungrazed pasture. A bench sheltered behind a wall beckoned us and we sat for a while looking out across to the mainland as people must have done for centuries. Although the industry is much reduced, there is still some fishing here, small craft catching mainly lobsters and crabs. The most popular delicacy on the island is, in fact, crab sandwiches, advertised across the island and probably so fresh the crabs were most likely caught that very day. Whilst sitting, we watched a little fishing boat heading into the bay, stopping right in front of us a few hundred yards away. The fishermen anchored up, unloaded their catch on to a little tender and set off to the harbour. We made our way to the harbourside, where their catch was being unloaded to a waiting van.

Malc spoke to the skipper: "What is it you are unloading?"

"Crabs and lobsters" came the reply.

"Have you had a good catch?" Malc continued.

"Not bad." He was a man of few words, but then he was busy!

"Where is it you are sending it to?" said Malc, undeterred.

"Up to Eyemouth, up beyond Berwick-upon-Tweed. Most of it will be sent to the continent. People in Britain aren't really interested in them, so we send them abroad."

Fishermen apparently don't need to sail far to find their catch. They are often able to stay in the bay itself, so obviously crabs and lobsters are found in large numbers here just offshore. Just further down the mainland coast, children enjoy crabbing in the sea from the harbour wall with their crab lines and buckets. Not quite big enough to eat though!

Now I really must come back to Cuthbert. What was it that made him so loved, revered and venerated? Bede, a monk who lived not far away at Monkwearmouth, and who lived around the same time, is famous not for healing or council, but for another talent common amongst medieval monks – writing. His famous book *The Ecclesiastical History of the English People* is probably the greatest source of information about the life and times of people and Christianity in Saxon times. He knew Cuthbert and wrote about him warmly and affectionately. He said that his faith shone out of him and he had a kind human touch which drew people to him.

Like Hilda of Whitby, Cuthbert was revered as a great counsellor, someone people sought out for advice, comfort and prayer. He was a great leader too. After the famous Synod of Whitby, Cuthbert, who was a fervent adherent of the Celtic Christian tradition, nevertheless took on board responsibility for its outcome. This meant changing the whole emphasis of his abbey, as well as the minds of his fellow monks, to that of the Roman Church, not an easy task, and, although successful, he must have faced much opposition. Over the years, Cuthbert also developed a reputation as a healer, which increased after his death.

When he died in AD 687 at the age of fifty-three he was buried on his beloved Lindisfarne. After Cuthbert had been dead for ten years his coffin was opened. This seemed to be something of a tradition at the time. The bones would be removed, cleaned and reburied. However, in the case of Cuthbert, when his coffin was opened he was revealed to be still entire. His body was found to be totally uncorrupted – a great marvel. As a result, Cuthbert's reputation grew once again. His body became a powerful focus for pilgrims, different from when he was alive. They came to revere him and to seek healing. Touching his shrine and belongings was said to allow his eminence to manifest itself in healing.

But Cuthbert was not allowed to rest in peace. Viking incursions and plundering were prevalent, and everywhere along the coast felt insecure and threatened. Eventually the monks felt obliged to leave not just the abbey, but the island. But they were not going without Cuthbert. His coffin was carried with them along with the head of King Oswald (I'm not sure where the rest of his body was!), and they set off to find a new and more secure place to live. In fact, they wandered for 200 years, carrying Cuthbert still, even though generations of the monks had never known him. For a while they stayed at Chester-le-Street in County Durham, but then continued to wander. Finally, Cuthbert and the monks came to rest in Durham City itself, and here in 999 they stayed at last in a permanent home. They were given land on a spur on the River Wear.

Cuthbert's reputation lived on and Durham with its abbey and cathedral grew to become one of the most powerful cities in the north. The cathedral became a final resting place for Cuthbert and his shrine is there still. Lindisfarne, even though monks returned, was never again an independent religious house; it became an outpost of Durham, its reputation poor, and it slowly declined as fewer and fewer monks wished to live there.

In general, Cuthbert had never cared about worldly wealth, but the sheer number of pilgrims during his lifetime had brought untold wealth and prosperity to his abbey. When his coffin was again opened at Durham some exquisite artefacts were found inside. Two were particularly beautiful: a gold pectoral cross with a garnet at its centre, and a silver travelling altar, which he took with him on his journeys to meet and worship with his many followers. Archaeologists were amazed at the skill needed to forge these items, for it is generally believed that such skills were not evident in the Dark Ages. Perhaps they weren't so dark as we thought!

It seems sad to me that Cuthbert was never returned, and a shrine built at Lindisfarne. He did not belong to Durham, so it would have been fitting to return him 'home', especially since it is still on Holy Island where Cuthbert is most remembered and where people still come to 'find' him, to retreat, to meditate and to understand the world and the place he knew.

Yet there is still more to this little island.

With their ability to read and write and with developing skills in creating manuscripts, monks in many places across Britain and the rest of Europe produced beautiful painted Gospels. The Book of Kells is famous, but the Lindisfarne Gospels are equally so, and possibly they are earlier too. Whilst copies can be seen on the island, the originals are now in the British Library. Probably written in the eighth century (this was after Cuthbert), their great beauty and the skill required meant they took ten years to complete, and this magnificent work of art was probably undertaken by just one man, a monk at Lindisfarne. The beauty of both the writing and the paintings seems even more poignant when realising it was worked on only in candlelight and spluttering, probably smelly oil lamps – a work quite simply of devotion and dedication. It is a realisation which takes your breath away.

Before setting off to come home, Malc and I went down to the start of the causeway. There has not always been a causeway, but there has been for many centuries a way across the sands. Known as

Cuthbert's Way, this was a pilgrim route, relatively safe as long as you were sensible. Markers in the form of long stakes were buried in the sand, and these marked the route, but even at low tide it was probably an uncomfortable walk with large puddles and mud along the way. In my imagination I could envisage stretched-out lines of pilgrims making their way, some alone, others, like Chaucer's pilgrims, in groups. They could be raucous, excited, seeing their journey as an adventure. Some would carry large wooden crosses. Some people would, no doubt, be carried by friends as they came to seek healing. Some would hobble along, fearful of not making it at all. And all the time they would be surrounded by so much sand, mud, thousands of seabirds, and seals watching from a distance. And stakes, such an important guide across the wilds of mudflats, are still there, and there are still pilgrims today who choose to walk this way to the island, leaving the twentieth century behind, preferring this old traditional method of reaching this sacred Holy Island. The stakes don't quite follow the line of the modern causeway. As you drive along you see the stakes disappear as they follow a different trajectory to the mainland. Past and present are still conjoined, with people today still seeking the same things in life as did those early pilgrims. We think we are so different today, sophisticated, modern, all-knowing, yet inside we all still seek that same inner peace and some understanding of life and the world, looking for the answers which give cohesion and comfort to our spirit. We may not find, but we will continue to seek.

On our way home we took time to rest by the River Tweed, that great and famous Border salmon river. At almost the end of its journey to the sea it opens up on to its wide, flat plain as it flows to Berwick-upon-Tweed. Its importance as a salmon river is still paramount, and it is the ambition of so many fishermen to fish its famous waters.

We both contemplated a little on our recent visit. Certainly I still felt the presence of Cuthbert there. Of course most people who visit don't come because of him, or even because of the island's great ecclesiastical importance. Yet residents do still uphold the importance of their saint. This does help to reinforce the feeling that Cuthbert and what he stood for are still tangible.

Cuthbert's Isle, a tiny island a short distance from Holy Island itself, where Cuthbert retreated for prayer and meditation. The cross marks the spot where Cuthbert built a small chapel.

Lindisfarne Harbour with huts made from upturned old fishing boats.

Ruins of the abbey at Holy Island on a bright but very cold day.

Sculpture in the island church of Lindisfarne, representing monks of the eighth century carrying the coffin of St Cuthbert, when fleeing from the Vikings.

Statue of St Cuthbert in the abbey grounds.

Marilyn walking the traditional St cuthbert's Way, where pilgrims would walk the path across sand and mudflats from the mainland to Holy Island.

St Cuthbert Cross

ST CUTHBERT FINALLY COMES TO REST:
ST CUTHBERT AT DURHAM

Following the line of Hadrian's Wall, the A69 goes across country west to east, from Carlisle to Newcastle. It's a lovely and an easy drive for us. There is a section where many large mature beech trees line the road. On a late September day when we were travelling their leaves were russet and beautiful in the autumn sunshine.

The turn-off for Durham is before Newcastle, and as we drove gaily along I suddenly said to Malcolm, "Can you turn right here?"

"Why?" he answered confusedly. "Durham is straight on!"

"Yes, I know, but I'd like to go to this village on the right."

"OK, but why?"

"Because it's Lanchester."

This was not an answer for him, but it was for me so I explained it. I was a student in Coventry in the West Midlands. Prior to going there I did not know the area at all, but I came to really love Coventry, a large city with a history of weaving and then manufacturing and heavy industry. It felt like a place of optimism. During the Second World War Coventry had been heavily bombed, and one of its casualties was the lovely old cathedral. After the war, Coventry picked itself up and rebuilt itself. When I first went there I was impressed by what must have been one of the first modern shopping precincts and traffic-free walkways. The bombed-out cathedral, however, was not rebuilt. Its ruins were cleared and left as a testament to the city's history. Instead, a brand-new, modern, state-of-the-art cathedral was built directly opposite the ruins. Beautiful, unique and ultra-modern, it became very much a tourist attraction, putting Coventry on the map. People were curious about this new cathedral and very impressed by it.

I was a student at the 'Lanchester', fondly known as the Lanch. Lecture theatres and student accommodation directly faced the cathedral frontage, with its famous sculpture of Archangel Michael. Almost every day I would walk the path past the two cathedrals on my way into the city. But why the Lanchester? The answer lies in Coventry's massive car and cycle industry. In the industry's heyday there were some 130 car, ninety motorcycle and 300 bicycle manufacturers in Coventry.

So it wasn't this village, however, after which the Lanch was named. Twentieth-century Coventry flourished on the car industry and was known as the motor city of the UK. There were hundreds of manufacturers, ranging from cycles and motorcycles to cars, including the highly esteemed Rolls-Royce and Jaguar, and support industries making car accessories. This industrial flourishing was reflected in the wages of car workers, who were paid twenty-five per cent more than the national average.

The first four-wheel petrol-driven car produced in Britain, in 1895 was manufactured by the talented brothers Frederick and George Lanchester, both of whom were engineers. Following its success, they founded the Lanchester Motor Company in 1899. It is unclear where the family originated, but certainly they lived early on in Birmingham and built their cars in Coventry, becoming part of its early illustrious history.

It is therefore this link with the Lanchester family, and the car named after them, which led to the college being named in their honour. Although now called simply Coventry University, the Lanchester name has not been forgotten. The university holds the archive on Frederick Lanchester, and his heritage lives on.

More recently, the university has been promoting the idea of the Lanchesters being depicted on a banknote. Although not a household name, it is a shame they should not be more widely remembered as the pioneer manufacturers they were.

These days the only truly British-owned and -made car is the Morgan.

The list of locally built cars in the transport museum is something of which the city is proud, and at the same time a very sad reflection on the British car industry of the present day. The Lanchester was one such car. Its name is the same as the village we had just passed in Durham. It still is a small village, with the village green dotted with mature trees and a few shops. It is nothing spectacular, but it is nice and I was glad to have seen it, making a link from so many years ago.

The student coincidence re-emerged when we arrived in Durham City. The cathedral and castle stand above the River Wear, in a commanding position on a spur of rock high above, giving the building a prominence and majesty on the Durham skyline. Also, around the cathedral closes and lanes are the university buildings, Durham being an old well-established and esteemed red-brick university. And quite unknowingly we arrived on the weekend of the first day of term. Of course it was a hive of activity, students and parents with cases and backpacks were everywhere, as they arrived to find their accommodation. Groups of excited students sat around on the grass in the cathedral close, excited on finding friends and fellow students whom they hadn't seen since the previous term. Narrow lanes led down into town, the pubs, cafés and bars busy and full of excited chatter as students and families took advantage of some refreshment, mostly of the alcoholic type.

Throughout all this, the cathedral just stood and took it all in its stride. After all, it has stood in this spot for over 1,000 years, and there isn't much it hasn't seen.

This solid sandstone structure has been classed as possibly the most awesome Norman cathedral in Britain, and it has always attracted visitors and admirers. Today, being in the heart of a large north-east urban area, it continues to attract. Inside it is famous for its nave of thick, red, solid, carved sandstone pillars. The day we visited it was busy too, no doubt numbers swelled by thousands of returning and new students and their families. And yet, despite its acclaimed grandeur, it is its famous long-term resident I have come to find.

It was at Lindisfarne where we first came across the revered Cuthbert. There he lived, died and was buried on his beloved Lindisfarne, but he was not allowed to rest there in peace. Viking incursions were happening right across Britain at this time, Danes in the east and south, and Norsemen (probably from Norway) in Scotland and Ireland.

The *Anglo-Saxon Chronicle* has a record of the Norsemen attacking Lindisfarne around 793: 'The heathen miserably destroyed God's church in Lindisfarne by rapine and slaughter.'

Hopefully with some advance warning, the monks of the abbey were able to escape, whereupon their exile began. These attacks continued, and it was in 794 that Northumberland was apparently ravaged and the monastery at Jarrow too was looted.

Amidst all this turmoil, the monks abandoned their abbeys. At Lindisfarne they prepared to leave, and they set out on a journey to an unknown destination. Effectively they were exiles, and they can't ever have imagined that it would be 200 years before a final refuge, at Durham, was found. These monks, however, were not going without their beloved Cuthbert, determined not to leave him at the mercy of the Vikings. He was once again disinterred, the monks, no doubt, taking turns to carry his simple wooden coffin, also containing the head of King Oswald. Where the rest of Oswald's body lay I don't know, but Oswald was going with them too, whether he wanted to or not! So for 200 years they wandered, staying here and there, surviving on what people and other religious houses could give them. At one point they rested for a considerable time at Chester-le-Street in County Durham and a St Cuthbert's Church is still there. Having been forced from their homes, and with the added burden of Cuthbert, they must have wondered if they could ever be at rest. Their faith was strong and they still believed he would rescue them. In the end their journey took far longer than Moses and the Israelites' trek of forty years in the desert. Eventually they were welcomed at Durham in 999, and from this event Durham's cathedral grew and prospered with Cuthbert as its revered saint.

Although unexpected exiles, these monks reflected the earliest pilgrim tradition, which changed over time. The word pilgrim is derived from *peregrini* (to wander), and these *peregrini* set off on their peregrinations.

When early Christians devoted themselves to the missionary cause they set off on their travels, knowing they would probably never return to their own home. The intention was to set out perhaps a bit aimlessly and go in any direction in which they felt drawn by God. During these peregrinations they would preach and convert, living as itinerant preachers with no home, no income and no possessions, often dependent on charity. They were rolling stones. Sometimes they would put down roots and eventually remain in this one place for the rest of their lives. St Kentigern and St Columba are good examples of these early *peregrini*. They could be very extreme journeys too.

The story of St Brendan, now believed not to be just a legend, is one such. With a few companion monks, Brendan set off from Ireland in a coracle. He related some of his adventures, and his words seem to indicate that they ultimately made it right across the Atlantic as far as America! Fanciful?

Then the nature of the pilgrim changed. It became the action of faithful Christians of all social classes to want to visit sites made famous by the miraculous events of the lives of saints. Initially, and with the example of the Crusades, those with a fervent faith, with money and opportunity, wanted to go to Jerusalem and to see for themselves the places described to them by those returning from the Holy Land.

Further development led to pilgrimage becoming a popular idea; and with many local pilgrim sites and established pilgrim routes, pilgrimage became an ever popular activity in the Middle Ages, filling many needs – healing, advice, company and holiday. It became the first example of the tourist trade, and everyone wanted to go.

And Durham, after Cuthbert came to rest here, became a major pilgrim destination. An old characterful medieval city, today it is impressive and respected, and yet at the same time the cathedral and castle are remnants of those early times, when it grew by the river in a position which both protected it and emphasised its importance. It was then a rural enclave, and in total contrast to the area surrounding the city and the county today as well as much of the north-east.

It was during the Industrial Revolution that this area was transformed, moving from rural industry and farming to one of the largest urban landscapes in the country. Industry grew and manufacturing increased too, especially in iron and steel, railways, canals and shipbuilding, and all of this was built on coal.

I was interested to find out a little about the coal industry, especially since I hail from Wigan in the heart of the Lancashire coalfields. Both Durham and Lancashire had extensive coalfields, Durham's stretching in a triangle down to Darlington, across the coast of Middlesbrough and Sunderland, up beyond Newcastle and into Northumberland. Looking at the landscape around Durham I felt it was very similar to that around Wigan and Lancashire: relatively flat, dumpy, quite ordinary. No doubt the coal seams underground create a similar above-ground look.

There are, of course, many other similarities, not least the devastation coal mining had on the land. Virtually whole counties experienced serious degradation, with unsightly pit-heads across the area, endless slag heaps, often still smoking, and flashes (created ponds by the slag heaps, made from flushed-out mine water). Then there was the pollution and coal-laden barges discharging coal dust into the atmosphere and fallen coal into the canal water. It was not a pretty sight. It may not have been the prettiest of countryside, but it was manifestly worse when the industry was at its height. And of course coal was like gold during the Industrial Revolution, so much depended on it. Nor are we talking of just a few mines! In 1898, the Durham and Northumberland coalfield had 358 mines. In the same year, Lancashire was not far behind with 327. The industry continued to expand. In Durham in 1880 71,852 people worked in the mines both above and below the ground. This increased to 165,807 in 1913, after which the industry started to decline.

Coal created major wealth. Pit owners and owners of the land on which the pitheads stood became some of the wealthiest people. Of course landownership had always provided security and money to Britain's large landowners. But now what was under the land was a new and easy way to make ever more wealth. Some landowners set up their own pits and extracted the coal. Others leased their land, whilst others excavated and paid rent and royalty to the landowner. Many famous landowners benefited in this way. The family of the Queen Mother, the Bowes-Lyon family, had a major stake in coal mining; the dean and chapter of Durham Cathedral also grew rich receiving royalties on lands owned by the church.

In Lancashire, the Gerard family of Bryn, near Wigan, had lived and held land there for many centuries. This was the old esteemed family to which the martyr St Edmund Arrowsmith belonged.* The Gerards suddenly found that their land sat on some of the richest coal seams in Lancashire, and Lord Gerard as a result became enormously wealthy.

And through all these changing centuries and fortunes, the cathedral in Durham has lived to tell the tale. Its reputation ensures its perennial popularity with visitors, and heavily populated North-East England also produces a steady flow. On the day we were there it was busy.

Yet, as beautiful and famous as it is, it was not the building itself which had brought me here. Rather, it was St Cuthbert. I wanted to see him at rest after his long exile, but I also wanted to view his sacred belongings, now displayed in a brand-new state-of-the-art exhibition in Durham Cathedral.

When Cuthbert's body was disinterred and translated his coffin was found to hold some exquisite items, presumably buried with him. These artefacts are extremely valuable and it is a testament to his 'minders', many of whom never even knew Cuthbert, that they were kept safe for 200 years. When modern archaeologists studied them, they were astounded at their beauty, value and exceptional craftsmanship. As an ascetic, Cuthbert would not have cared or yearned for possessions, yet due to his own special attributes his Lindisfarne Abbey became wealthy. He was buried with his gold

* See 'St Edmund's Hand', page 174.

pectoral cross, a garnet at its centre. It is a beautiful ornately detailed piece of religious artwork. He also had a small travelling altar made of pure solid silver. These were not superfluous status-affirming pieces. Rather, they were part and parcel of his faith. His cross would have been worn on his travels and visits and the altar would have been carried with him to provide an aid and symbol during worship away from Lindisfarne, on his missionary or other duties. His original wooden coffin also survives, but it is incomplete. These are the items which now comprise the new Cuthbert exhibition.

Overall, our experience of the cathedral and the exhibition was not a good one, a real disappointment. The cathedral prides itself on not having an entrance fee, and in general this is laudable as most cathedrals need approximately £4,000 per day for their upkeep. However, Durham did not have a particularly welcoming feel, and, judging by later comments on TripAdvisor, we were not alone. Money seemed to be a priority in lots of other ways. It was £5 for a guidebook, £5 to go up into the tower, £5 for a guided tour and a further £7.50 to see the new exhibition. At the same time volunteers around the cathedral were handing out leaflets encouraging people to go on through to see Cuthbert's exhibition. Photography was not allowed, full stop. Yes, of course it is a house of God, but equally its impressive architecture and history are also the reason many people come. Not everyone who comes is a practising Christian, but they want to see this beautiful building and also like to take photographs as mementos of the day. We saw several people being told not to take photographs and then heard many people expressing their dismay. They were genuinely upset. At Carlisle visitors paid £2 to take as many pictures as they want.

As with many important shrines, Cuthbert was buried behind the high altar, and body does lie below, but there is no sense of how it must have been when this place was brimming with pilgrims in the Middle Ages.

Moving to the new exhibition wee paid our £7.50, after all, this was partly why we had come. There were two separate elements. The first was a rather unoriginal display of stonework, old stone crosses, an interactive display and copies of the Ruthwell and

Bewcastle Cross, both Anglian. However, it is very easy to see these original crosses in situ at Ruthwell and Bewcastle, where it costs nothing at all.

Cuthbert's exhibition was in a separate small, almost circular room with a lovely vaulted roof, which seemed intimate and gave me a feeling of anticipation. Mistake! This anticipation soon evaporated on seeing the layout of Cuthbert's fabulous artefacts. We noticed that few people had actually paid to come through to this new exhibition. Their interest in Cuthbert was not important enough to warrant paying the high entrance fee? Durham Cathedral attracts people knowing that its wonderful Norman architecture is worth making the journey to see. Yet these days the cathedral seems to have adopted Cuthbert as its symbol and promotes him as the reason to come. In my humble opinion, however, this didn't to me seem to be people's motivation, irrespective of the new exhibits. I don't think there were many Cuthbert pilgrims there the day I visited.

To me, Cuthbert's exhibition was completely wrong, its design seemingly to me not in keeping with Cuthbert. He would not I think have been impressed, and neither was I. Cuthbert's artefacts are exquisite, but small. They need also to be seen not just as pieces to be displayed, but should reflect their owner, his faith and personality. Displayed separately, his cross and altar were in huge display cabinets, behind brightly lit glass with ninety-nine per cent empty space. His cross sat alone and bewildered in a superfluity of glass and totally dwarfed by it. Not only that, but it was set so high up; a minuscule speck, that I at five feet tall couldn't even see it. The same went for his silver altar. Having photocopies displayed around the room was not a substitute for the real thing. What are they thinking?

Cuthbert's much disintegrated wooden coffin was in another glass case. Why they couldn't just leave it and let people walk around and look at it from all sides, I don't know. But no, it was somehow flashed and flipped around from one side to another. We don't need to be entertained with flashing lights and reams of glass; we just wanted to be able to see it! That's why we came.

On top of all this, there was nothing to tell us about Cuthbert, to put it all into context with his life and times. To me they have missed the opportunity to tell the story of a greatly venerated saint, his experiences and his faith. Cuthbert doesn't exist as an owner of artefacts, they are only there as a facet of his extraordinary life and post-mortem journey. A unique man with beautiful and unique treasures, but not an exhibition just of treasures, please! And I still believe these beautiful items and Cuthbert himself should have gone back to Lindisfarne.

A MOST VENERATED SAINT: ST BEDE AT DURHAM

Like Cuthbert, the remains of the Venerable Bede lie in Durham Cathedral. Also like Cuthbert, Bede had no association with Durham or its cathedral, having been brought here many years after his death, supposedly in the early part of the eleventh century, having been translated by a Durham monk. Whether his bones were stolen or brought here for safekeeping is still a moot point. No one knows, but since that time he has rested peacefully in the cathedral, though he was moved into his own Galilee Chapel (having formerly shared with Cuthbert and King Oswald's head) when it was completed in the twelfth century.

For me this Galilee Chapel was possibly the loveliest part of the cathedral. It is visually stunning. The deeply incised chevron sculpting on the pillars and other intricate Norman decoration is fabulous. However, it is further interesting because it was built on the cusp of change from Norman to Early English architecture, which would come to be characterised by higher ceilings, soaring arches and larger windows. Whilst Norman in its decoration, it nevertheless felt more spacious and airy. Not many visitors had ventured in, so it was quiet, peaceful, reverent. I felt I was in the presence not just of a great man – Bede – but also God.

So, who was Bede? And why is he here and so revered? Certainly, his shrine wouldn't tell you: it is so understated it is very easy to miss it altogether!

Bede was a Saxon monk based all his life in the monastery of Monkwearmouth, near Newcastle upon Tyne, although some historians believe it was at Jarrow, the joint monastery. Living in the eighth century, he lived his whole life from seven years old here, hardly ever leaving it. If this seems like an hermitic existence, with no worldly knowledge, then this belies the truth. For Bede was a brilliant scholar; he devoted his life to learning, researching, writing and translating (mostly theological texts). Bede was the first person to translate St John's Gospel from Latin into the local language. It was finished, literally, on his deathbed, on 25 May 735.

He is most famously remembered for his book *The Ecclesiastical History of the English People*, written when he was fifty-nine years old. The importance of this book in respect of history cannot be overestimated. From this source we know so much about the northern Celtic Church and its saints, as well as being a general and theological history of England as Bede 'saw' it. Without his writings our knowledge of this period of history would be sparse indeed, throwing light as it does on Dark Age England. His skill was enhanced by the availability of books, texts and manuscripts, for his monastery was said to be particularly wealthy in these valuable assets. Also, visitors would bring more, adding to the collection over time, and his information was enriched by news-bearing guests and passing travellers. Hence we find familiar names, such as King Oswald, Aidan, Hilda and Wilfrid. Cuthbert we know he met and was fond of, speaking warmly of him. He was far from parochial, however, and he tells us of people and places not just in England, but across Europe. Nor was he averse to discussing issues and concerns close to his heart. As part of the Celtic Church, he speaks often about the debate concerning the date of Easter, which was at variance with that of the Roman Church and was a major issue at the Synod of Whitby.

Yet of Bede himself we know almost nothing. We know when he died, but not when he was born or where he came from. He was apparently admitted to the monastery at the age of seven.

Bede may not have travelled far in his life, but he was known, loved, respected and revered for his knowledge and skill, and when he died, in 731, a cult developed around him. As happened with Cuthbert, with the tradition of exhumation about ten years after death, Bede too was disinterred. Unlike Cuthbert, however, Bede was skeletonised, so his bones were washed and reinterred. It was at this point, when the bones were unearthed, that people around experienced healing. His relics then became a focus not just of reverence for his artistic skills, but for his power to heal. This power led to the establishment of a flourishing pilgrim trade to Monkwearmouth. Although now in ruins, the remaining church shows evidence of Saxon origins, parts of the church which Bede would have recognised. Pilgrimage was relatively short-lived here, and the reasons are unclear, but the probability is that Viking incursions, which were happening all along the east coast at this time, were the reason the monastery was abandoned, and it was never reoccupied.

What happened to his relics before being taken to Durham is unclear.

Today Bede is remembered and revered not for healing, but for his writings, and quite rightly so. His famous book is still in print, giving us an insight into those Saxon times.

A separate letter appears in the book, sent by a monk named *Cuthbert, a scriptorium student of Bede of whom he thought highly. He is writing to Cuthwin, whom we don't know, but who wanted to know about Bede's death. Cuthbert's love of Bede shines out in this letter. A few excerpts reflects this:

Praise for the Gospel of John, which he translated into our mother tongue. He wanted all to be able to read the real words of Jesus in their own language.

On the Tuesday before Ascension Day his breathing became very much worse and with a slight swelling on his feet. But he taught and dictated cheerfully:

"Learn your lesson quickly now, for I know not how long I

* Not the same St Cuthbert.

may be with you. . . ."

He had still one chapter of the Gospel to translate. Bede said, "Take your pen and write fast."

A boy, Wilberht, cried, "There is still one more sentence, dear master, that we have not written down." And Bede said, "Write it." The boy said, "It is written." Bede replied, "Good. It is finished."

And so, on the floor of his cell, singing, "Glory be to the Father and to the Son and to the Holy Spirit," he breathed his last.

All who heard or saw the death of our saintly father Bede declared that they had never seen a man end his days in such a great holiness and peace.

This lovely letter could have been written yesterday, with words and emotion just as in modern times. Clearly he was a man dearly loved and admired, and not just by those in his own monastery. Indeed, that respect is still greatly apparent today. We can still read his work and can also appreciate the extent of his skill and the depth of his emotion and devotion, seen in the love of his students and a faith which showed itself in his dedication to writing, translating and sharing his knowledge. All his life's work was his personal way of praising God and reveals his determination to tell others and bring them to the Christian faith by ensuring that people had access to the Bible.

Nor should we imagine that any of this was easy. Bede needed first to be able to read, write and understand (remember that at this time everything he read would have been in Latin or another foreign language), and he was a pioneer in translating works into the local evolving English language. Clearly he loved books and sought out new tracts to read, and such was his enthusiasm that many students wanted to learn from him. This was despite the slow, laborious, eye-straining task that was the life of a student in a scriptorium. The work produced in these monastic houses was no minor feat. So much we take for granted, now readily available, was not available then. There was no paper, no ink, no pens and no electric light. Even before starting to write Bede had to source his materials and then prepare them. There would be parchment, probably made from calfskin, quill pens made from feathers, ink made from oak galls and light provided by cheap candles (good candle wax was expensive) and often oil or butter lamps, which were smelly and smoky. If colour was needed, then this created another problem of learning what to use, where to find it and how to mix it. Pigments could be derived from plants, rocks and insects and were expensive. This was especially true for the Gospel illuminators, who needed expertise not just in writing but in art and the use of colour too. Overall it was a painstaking, difficult, often uncomfortable, highly skilled and lengthy job, with the end result sometimes many years in the making. Yet Bede's students clearly loved him and learned from him with patience and enthusiasm, knowing also that the end product would be one of which they could be proud. The work also provided opportunities for independence and flair, making up their own designs and colour schemes. A good example of this is found in the Lindisfarne Gospels. The writer is thought to have worked alone on his project for ten years before its completion. His colours and designs were all his own. When studying them, it was noticed that he did not use the colour gold in any of his intricate designs. Did he not like gold and chose not to use it? Or maybe he decided it was too expensive or too flamboyant.

But did they realise that so much of what they undertook would still be so beautiful and admired so many hundreds of years later?

Bede was not interested in wealth or self-glorification. Everything he did was done by and in faith. His tomb in Durham Cathedral is not lavish in decoration. It is a simple structure resting in a beautiful place of God, a quiet chapel where he lies in peace, knowing he did everything he could to glorify God and bring the word to whoever would listen and read.

NOTES:

2. *The Anglo-Saxon Chronicle* (793) reports on terrible

cataclysmic physical events. On 8 January we read of the harrying of the heathen (probably Norsemen), who miserably destroyed God's church at Lindisfarne accompanied by rapine and slaughter.

St Bede's Galilee Chapel chevron pillar.

A MODERN PILGRIMAGE TO A TOWN OF TRAGEDY: LOCKERBIE

Part One

I am visiting a town which, although pleasant, is small and unassuming. It is easy to bypass. Like many small towns it has a town hall and a sprinkling of shops and pubs along its main street, which like many other high streets is striving to maintain its identity and vibrancy. It has no outstanding features, no river running through, no large beautiful park and no marketplace. It is, however, surrounded by beautiful countryside of rolling hills. Yet this is a town which will be forever remembered against its will and wish. It has become known worldwide as the town of the air crash. For this is Lockerbie. The residents of Lockerbie now have to live with memories of a large airliner crashing on to the main road into the town from the south. Lockerbie cannot shed its fame. Rather, it lives with it in a quiet and unassuming way. Indeed, how could this little town ever forget the tragedy which befell it and for which it will always be remembered?

In December 1988, just a few days before Christmas, a Pan-Am jet took off from London heading to America and following a usual route. It turned left towards Lockerbie in South-West Scotland to head out into the Irish Sea. The plane never reached America – indeed, it barely reached Lockerbie. Blown up by a bomb in mid-air, it broke into two pieces. Facts later determined that it was only due to lateness taking off that the tragedy happened here. The bomber's intention was for the explosion to happen over the ocean.

The cockpit of the aircraft landed about two miles away in a field along with its crew. The body of the plane flew a little further, crashing in flames with all its passengers on a residential road only yards from the town centre. As well as the whole crew and passengers, ten people also died on the ground as the aircraft landed directly on homes, demolishing them and setting others ablaze. Today, families, pilgrims, visitors and the curious still come to Lockerbie. The monument to those who died is modest, as befits the little town, yet its effect is great. Indeed, it is probably its very simplicity that renders it into a memorial of overwhelming sadness. It has an atmosphere not just of total and acute sorrow and horror, but of terrible loss and the cruel and unnecessary loss of life. Many of the passengers were young, looking forward to spending Christmas with their families. All the passengers and crew should have had their lives, careers and futures ahead of them. The memorial bears witness to the overwhelming utter waste of human life.

You will find the monument in an old established cemetery on the outskirts of town, and it provides a quiet and peaceful spot for visitors. There are trees and woods all around, and just across the road is a nature reserve – a haven attracting visitors who come to see the red squirrels that thrive here.

The coachloads of visitors who swarmed here in the early days have inevitably thinned, but even so a steady stream of people still arrive, walking quietly to the memorial and then visiting the small visitor centre by the cemetery gates. In here they can learn more about the tragedy and its victims and can sign a book of condolence if they wish.

On the day I visited, an ordinary, slightly damp day in October, I strolled along the main path feeling, if I'm honest, a little apprehensive. I was right to be, for, although not buried here, the names of all those who died in the explosion, including Lockerbie residents, are recalled here. It is overwhelmingly sad and solemn. It is a moving and tearful experience, remembering all these hundreds of people. I didn't know any of the victims, but there were tears in my eyes nevertheless.

Another memorial, smaller and quite remote, lies beside a country church at Tundergarth, a tiny settlement. A plain small stone building commemorates those who fell at this spot, the pilots and cabin crew. The cone of the aircraft was separated from the rest and landed seconds before the main fuselage in the town.

For many months following the tragedy people living in surrounding areas beneath the flight path often found remnants of the plane and its contents on their land; unwanted reminders of those who died. Such physical reminders were a testament to the sheer force and horror of the blast. Less and less was uncovered over the years, but the truth is that the residents of Lockerbie do not need such physical reminders of that terrible day. It is a day they can never forget, and a sad legacy for an ordinary, small Scottish town.

In the visitor centre I spoke to the manager. I wanted to know who today's visitors are and how have things changed?

"People still come from all over the world, and in fact some of the more numerous are from Australia, Holland, Belgium and Germany," she told me. "Of course we still get many people who make a pilgrimage here. Many relatives come on special occasions, such as birthdays, as well as for specially convened memorial services; and even after so many years you can still clearly see the pain on people's faces as they remember the tragedy. It isn't something you can ever really forget. But", she added, "it is important to remember too that many people who have no association with Lockerbie still come to remember the tragedy which shocked the nation and indeed the world. They come to pay their respects and offer prayers for those who died and their families."

I asked her if the numbers who come had dropped.

"People no longer come in droves," she explained, "but they do come. There are many reasons why," she said.

But to me it was comforting to know that the victims of Lockerbie are not forgotten and hopefully never will be.

Before leaving, I signed the visitors book and clearly visitors are still international, coming from Japan, USA, Norway and New Zealand as well as England and Scotland, and were affected enough to want to sign the book as a sign of condolence and unity.

The only other people there when I visited were a family from Motherwell, near Glasgow. I asked them why they had come. They were in fact just passing through, but wanted to stop particularly so that their teenage daughter could see the memorial.

Before leaving Lockerbie, I decided to walk through the nature reserve, its entrance being literally across the road from the cemetery and providing a direct contrast. Eskrigg Nature Reserve is a lovely wooded area with many paths through the woods, with bird hides and a lake. This, in itself is pleasant, but most people come in the hope of seeing its most famous residents. This reserve is a haven for the now rare red squirrel, one of a few in the north of England and Scotland, where they are thriving.

Fortunately, you are almost guaranteed to see them, and what a delight they are! Much smaller than the grey, with a lovely face, tufted ears and a beautiful chestnut coat, it is entrancing to watch them flitting around on the ground, up and down and between trees. At the squirrel hide I saw many, and, although watchful for any danger, they were essentially unafraid.

I had had such a contrasting experience, from the sadness of the memorial to the beauty of nature and wildlife in close-up. And, too, the sound of laughter and the feeling of pleasurable anticipation as people waited to see the squirrels' arrival. The feeling here was of celebrating life, not the loss of it. Life in all its glory. Life is undoubtedly fleeting, sometimes tragic, but even in the footsteps of horror you can also see beauty and recognise and appreciate that life can and does go on.

Part Two

I didn't want in any way to detract from tragic pilgrimage experiences in this small town. However, when I initially realised the town may be Viking in origin, and named after the Norse god Loki, I thought this was interesting and delved a little deeper. Certainly there are other known Viking settlements in close proximity to Lockerbie, Torthorwald, Mousewald and Tinwald, so the town's link with the Norsemen is quite likely.

Loki was a minor god in Norse mythology, but he was a tiresome and irksome one. Although not truly or intrinsically evil, he had a reputation as a magician, a trickster and a shape-shifter. His trickery proved altogether too much when he killed the son of the great god Odin. For such a severe and unacceptable act, Odin took his revenge. He punished Loki by binding him in ropes, chains and padlocks and threw him into the underworld, where he was abandoned. Loki's end reflects and illustrates the idea of evil being banished to the dark, a sinister and evil underworld, whilst goodness is surrounded by light and life above ground. Good conquers evil. When the Vikings settled in Britain this metaphor became enmeshed with Christianity as the invaders became Christianised. Loki became the epitome of evil, the devil banished and defeated, to be forever subjugated in the dark underworld. Jesus became the Light, the Defeater of evil and the Saviour of the world.

I was drawn to this story when I discovered the existence of the Loki Stone, an ancient, rare and beautiful artefact.

Kirkby Stephen is a lovely small market town abutting the Yorkshire Dales in the Eden Valley of East Cumbria. Locals, however, still remember when this was another county, Westmorland, still remembered in the local Westmorland Show and *Westmorland Gazette* local newspaper. It is a beautiful spot, popular with tourists, with most visitors enjoying the traditional market and resting for lunch in the many cafés, then strolling down to the river. Most are probably unaware of the Loki Stone, now safely ensconced in the parish church, just off the Market Square. For such a small town the church is large and impressive with its many lovely and unusual characteristics. One of these is a bold granite and marble pulpit, extravagantly made and adorned around its perimeter with clear and traditional Masonic symbols. It was indeed paid for by the local Masonic lodge.

The church now functions as a joint place of worship for local Roman Catholics as well as Anglicans. The new vicar is also promoting the ethos of making the church a vibrant and integral part of town life, not just a place for Sunday worship. To this end, we watched volunteers erecting an exhibition of local artists' work.

One of the volunteers asked us if we would like to look at the paintings. "Do you think you could vote for your favourite?" she asked, and gave us a voting slip.

The quality was mixed, but we found one we really liked and put our vote in the box. Clearly it was an attempt to encourage people into the church, and also the artists would know people had taken an interest in their work.

But the focus of my visit called Malc and me back to the Loki Stone, in its prime position just inside the main door. It was much smaller than I had anticipated, but no less impressive for that. The carving was crisp and clear, and somewhat sinister, and it had been originally part of a Christian cross shaft of Viking/Christian origin. The rest of the shaft has been lost, and indeed it is only in relatively recent times that it has been placed in the church. For many years it lay in obscurity in the churchyard, and where it came from before that is a mystery hidden in the mists of time. What is known is that it was carved somewhere between the eighth and tenth centuries. The church guide describes the stone as an 'Anglo-Danish cross shaft engraved with the figure of a chained devil representing the god Loki. This is one of the very earliest Christian representations of the devil in a human form. This would seem to be a very north British concept, but it later spread across Europe as Scandinavians travelled and settled.'

What is even more amazing is that this is the only example so far found in Britain, with just one other in Europe. So how did such a stone end up in a quiet small town in Cumbria? No one knows. It is a mystery.

However, I found that a recent examination of a Pictish stone now in a museum in the Eastern Scottish Highlands appears to bear a striking similarity to the Loki Stone at Kirkby Stephen. Although not yet confirmed as such, it would add to the rare and valuable record of Norse carving in Britain.

Loki, it seems, provided a convenient example of a devil, which allowed for some clear iconography to be transferred from Norse mythology to the Christian faith. In those Dark Ages, it was important for Christians to visualise the defeated devil down in the dark bowels of the earth as compared to Jesus, the Saviour, glowing in celestial light and goodness. It was a clear message that goodness can and does overcome the evil of the world.

The world can still remember that evil was perpetrated in Lockerbie in 1988. But as Loki was able to create a positive from a negative, then so too let us hope that in memory and recognition of all who lost their lives we will see that the intrinsic and overriding goodness of humanity will overcome the evil in this world.

Loki Stone.

SAINTS, APPLES AND MISTLETOE
BOUGHS: HEREFORD

Malc and I would be the first to admit that our home town of
Wigan is not the prettiest, wealthiest or the most interesting.
Like many other people, I suspect, whilst we can criticise it,
we don't like non-Wiganers doing it! There was a well-known
saying when we were growing up there. Wigan's main road
artery is the A49, and we used to say that the only good thing
to come out of Wigan was the A49. Shame! It is a long road
of great scenic variety, and south of Wigan we followed it
from Cheshire right down to our destination at Symonds Yat in
Herefordshire. It was an easy relaxed journey, passing through
very affluent Cheshire on the flat, fertile and pretty Cheshire
Plain. Then the contrast came as we entered Shropshire, with
the lovely Shropshire hills. Finally, into Herefordshire and once
again a different landscape, hillier than Cheshire, flatter than
Shropshire. I know on a map where Herefordshire is, but find it
hard to describe. It isn't Southern England, nor is it the South
or West Midlands, but then neither is it really the West Country
either. It does seem to be somewhere on its own with its distinct
character and history. If anything, it would be like Shropshire, a
border county in the Welsh Marches, its history defined by the
many skirmishes, battles and wars with the Welsh.

The River Wye is its famous river, and it was on the banks
of this river where we stayed in Symonds Yat, a popular place
for visitors, including the Yat itself. The Yat, in East Symonds

Yat, is a huge rock, a landmark in the area. And a rock it is, not a hill or a crag or an inland cliff. It is very definitely a rock. At 500 feet it doesn't indicate that it is imposing, but its uniqueness lies in the fact that it is vertically straight from the ground, spectacularly sheer, steep, but its surface softened with woodland, ferns, wildflowers, and the fact that the view from the top provides a rolling vista of countryside and especially the river. Our hotel, formerly a royal hunting lodge, nestled literally under the rock overhang. It was in a beautiful spot, even in a dismal November.

We were only a few miles from the city of Hereford, my main destination and a city with a turbulent past. Hereford's county, of which it is the capital, is large and predominantly rural, with even Hereford having a population of only 60,000. Driving around, you can still see much of its traditional commerce, that of growing apples and the making of cider. The whole county has only 200,000 residents, and it describes itself as remote and unspoilt. A good description, I would say! I was looking forward to seeing the city, which still retains its medieval streets, with its heart being the River Wye and its wonderful cathedral, which stands by the riverbank.

Many visitors come specifically to see two of the cathedral's unique treasures. One is the chained library, where many rare and precious and very old books are kept. In the past, even when not old, books were nevertheless prized objects; and in order to prevent damage and, even more important, theft, the books were chained together as a protection. Such chained libraries are a rarity today. Yet the other item is even older and rarer. The Mappa Mundi is a map of the world created in the 1300s with the Holy Land and Jerusalem at the centre. It is now part of an exhibition showing and explaining its importance.

Others come, I'm sure, just to see this magnificent cathedral. Unlike some others, such as York or Durham, this cathedral is not throbbing with visitors and it was great to walk around in quiet and peace and appreciate its reverential atmosphere.

Of course this peaceful scene has not always existed. Like other places, it suffered greatly in the turbulent times of continued battles with the Welsh. It was severely damaged in 1056 and today it must stand relieved that times are quieter and that it is safe and secure at last.

The cathedral exterior does not have the flamboyance of soaring spires and intricate Gothic detail, but it has rather beautiful Norman architecture, which, although more muted, nevertheless is equally detailed and exuberant when looked at closely. Once inside, the place is rendered exquisite, at least to me. It is a truly beautiful church, predominantly Norman. The intricate Norman decorative carvings on pillars, arches and windows are outstanding, and an uncommon pattern is the distinctive 'ball flower' decoration. Strategic lighting, subdued but highly effective, is used to highlight and enhance areas of particular beauty. Unlike Durham's pillars of sandstone, the ones at Hereford are of grey stone, but they are not sombre.

On first considering Hereford for a pilgrimage I didn't realise that there are in fact two shrines, so I got more than I bargained for. Hereford's patron saint is Ethelbert, a king and a Saxon martyr. There must have been an earlier Saxon church because, although he lived before the present cathedral was built, it is known that he was buried in Hereford. As the cathedral, in parts, dates from the eighth century, then Ethelbert was a true Saxon king. His relics quickly became a focus for pilgrims and his cult survived for many centuries, until the twelfth century, when he was probably superseded by the second saint, St Thomas of Cantilupe. Of course, the truth about the lives of so many of these early saints is hard to verify. But in the case of St Ethelbert, there is written evidence of him, so the probability is that at least some of the facts are true.

The *Anglo-Saxon Chronicle* is an extremely important reference source for facts about people and places in these times. Thought to have been written between the ninth and twelfth centuries by unnamed monks, it tells of people and events important in these times and before; and, like Bede's book, it is an invaluable source of information. It is in this 'Chronicle' that we read about Ethelbert, and, although brief, it tells of his legend. Ethelbert would appear to have offended the famous King Offa of the Mercian kingdom* and the *Anglo-Saxon Chronicle* says this of him: 'Offa, King of the Mercians commanded the head of King Ethelbert to be struck off.'

His story was further elaborated over time, reinforcing his martyrdom. When his followers and retainers recovered his decapitated body, they lifted it on to a cart to carry it into Hereford. In a macabre twist, his head supposedly rolled off the cart into the mud. Searching for it, it was found by a blind man, who rescued it and returned it for burial. As a result, this man's sight was miraculously restored. Where the King's head reputedly fell a spring emerged, giving healing powers. When he was interred in the cathedral, pilgrims came to his shrine and healing continued. He was awarded his sainthood and his shrine became a flourishing pilgrim site.

Today nothing remains of his relics or his shrine, but a lovely tableau of images where his shine used to be tells his story. His shrine was in the Lady Chapel, and it is here that the oldest stained-glass windows in the cathedral are found, dating from the thirteenth century, although these were originally in another Hereford church. I think we all appreciate the glory and beauty of stained glass. It is so integral to the fabric of the church, but its purpose and history is something we often overlook.

Sir Roy Strong says that stained-glass windows stem from God creating light: 'God said, Let there be light: and there was light.' "The art of stained glass", he says, "stems from this association of spirituality with light."

There was an explosion of coloured glass created in medieval churches, moving on from the enhancement of light to using coloured glass to tell Bible stories and to create pictures of the saints. Of course, so many people were illiterate that they needed these visual aids to teach them about the Bible; it was a learning and very spiritual experience. Today very little medieval stained glass remains, much having been destroyed in the Reformation of the sixteenth century and also through decay and dereliction. Yet it is as popular now as ever, and so many places, along with Hereford Cathedral, show a history through their windows, their

* Mercia covered much of Midland England.

ages and styles and subject matter encapsulating the art and beauty of so many centuries.

We had to find the café, of course, but after suitable refreshment we took ourselves off and into the city.

Herefordshire is famed for its beautiful black-and-white villages and there is even a special trail around the loveliest. There were many black-and-white Tudor houses in the area, including Hereford itself, but over time these have been lost. One striking example still remains, however. Called simply the Black and White House, it stands in the centre of Hereford's main shopping area, reflecting how little its layout has changed over the centuries. This house is the last of what was a row of similar buildings known as Butchers' Row. This last magnificent remaining example is now a museum. This butcher must have been a wealthy and important man, for this house is large and impressive as I'm sure its owner meant it to be. Such merchants were the rich middle class of the day. It was built in the 1620s and still contains many original features, especially original wall paintings, currently being restored, which was the reason why much of the museum was closed. The steward told us that because of this entrance was free. Normally it was only a nominal £2.50.

"I suppose it must be quieter, then, with restricted access," I said to the steward.

"Actually, it's the opposite," he replied. "We've had lots of people coming in because it's free!"

'We don't change, do we?' I thought to myself. 'We do like to get something for nothing.' At £2.50 it is cheap, but people hesitate to pay it; then because it's free they will go and see it. There is a message there, I think. Would more people go to all those expensive galleries and museums if the entrance fee was more affordable? Undoubtedly!

We drove back to our hotel and once again saw something which seemed a mystery to me. I had noticed before that many trees seemed to have huge festoons of spheres of foliage hanging from the branches. The trees were leafless, yet masses of greenery hung incongruously from so many different trees. I had never seen anything like this before.

"What is this?" I kept asking Malc, who had no answers for me.

It was everywhere, mostly high up in the trees in profusion and hanging in elegant roundels. Then I realised.

"Malc, it's mistletoe!"

And indeed it was. Mistletoe, I know, doesn't grow in the North. If it does, it is rare, so seeing it in such abundance was a real sight to me. Sad, I know, but I found myself really enchanted at seeing it, for it is of course a plant of legend. We associate it with Christmas, a hanger-on from pagan times because it is also closely linked with the Druids. Celtic legend tells us about these famous and mysterious priests who revered the mistletoe above most other plants, apart from the oak tree. Where they found it they would climb ladders and then cut the mistletoe bough with a golden sickle. Whether any of this is true no one knows. The Romans wrote of the Druids, but exactly who they were and what their traditions were is still debated. In fact, there is only one extant historical record, written by Pliny in ancient times. All subsequent theories have been based on this single written record. Druids apparently worshipped in glades and loved trees, and the oak tree above all others. Yet mistletoe growing on oak is rare indeed. So it was probably this rarity which made it so special. In fact, mistletoe's favourite tree is the apple, which explains its abundance in this area with its tradition of apple orchards and cider making. It is a parasitic plant, but even at Christmas time it is still green with translucent white berries, reminiscent of valuable pearls. Often linked to the tradition of Yule, it is associated with holly and ivy. All of these plants remain green.

Before and during the Dark Ages, people revered evergreen plants and trees. It was a reminder that even in the depths of darkest winter days there are still green leaves, indicating the continuation of life and giving hope that spring will come again, bringing warmth and the growing of food. These evergreen branches would be brought into the house, a harbinger of spring.

At the beginning of December a local auction is held where those with mistletoe on their land can sell it. Thereby, it travels onward across the country for all to enjoy at Christmas, especially the romantic kisses under the mistletoe bough. Why does that seem such a lovely word, bough? It somehow reminds me of ancient times and old traditions which have come down to us through the centuries. Seeing the mistletoe, am I feeling that connection with our ancient pagan selves? Change is permanently with us, and yet, remarkably, there is still a great continuity of culture, myth and tradition, which is still part of life today. Christmas remains a mixture of so many things which somehow all meld together in our celebrations, where, hopefully, the primary celebration is that of the coming of Jesus to earth.

The next day, back in Hereford, we were strolling round the city, in and out of the old narrow closes, walking by the river and through open spaces, noticing the city's quirky characteristics. These include many examples of wrought iron, principally forming lovely intricate balconies on the Georgian houses in the old town. Then it was back to the cathedral and the story of Thomas de Cantilupe.

St Ethelbert was good for Hereford, making the city popular and bringing in money, prestige and recognition. But times change people and their ideas, and priorities come and go. Ethelbert remains the patron saint, but by the thirteenth century the town's favourite saint had been superseded by another more recent one, Thomas de Cantilupe. But then maybe Thomas gave Ethelbert a well-earned rest from his centuries of healing! He was a more recent saint, but, sad to say, his shrine did not fare much better, although as a result of pure chance it could have been much worse.

In 1275 Thomas was Bishop of Hereford, but by all accounts he was a man of strong opinions and a lover of theological debate. When he debated with the then Archbishop of Canterbury he chose the wrong debating opponent. The Archbishop was incensed that Thomas had the nerve and disrespect to argue with him. Thomas hadn't done anything wrong, but the Archbishop as head of the English Church excommunicated him, a somewhat harsh treatment. This was a devastating blow to Thomas, for it meant a catastrophic end to the life he knew, his position, power, income and security. The worst thing possible was to be excommunicated, for it could easily lead to him being damned, his soul lost forever. Thomas desperately needed absolution, and with friends and supporters he set off for Rome to see the Pope. An audience was granted and on hearing Thomas's story he granted him absolution and restored him to his former position. Sadly, before he even set off back home, he became ill and died in Rome, from where his friends brought his body back to Hereford. Here he was buried. Almost immediately he was found to have healing power for those who came to visit his shrine in the cathedral. From this time pilgrims visited in great numbers.

Throughout this book I have stressed the popularity of pilgrimage and how large numbers, especially in the Middle Ages, visited the many pilgrim sites, but what do we mean by large numbers? It is a vague statement, and generally there were no registers kept of who came and went. However, Hereford Cathedral does have some records, particularly regarding the amount of money raised from pilgrims. From the figures, it is possible to extrapolate a rough guess as to the numbers visiting in any one year. The cathedral guide tells us that in 1290–91 the amounts donated totalled £286 1s. 8½d. Today's equivalent would be around £200,000 – a staggering amount. All pilgrims would probably give both money and gifts. On this basis, even if each pilgrim gave a penny then the visitor numbers for that year could have been as many as 30,000. Some pilgrims would give more, reducing the total, and some would come more than once, but, even so, this too is a huge number. They brought gifts too, votives, objects in wood and even silver, placed on the shrine. Crutches were left as a sign of healing; silver cribs were left by those requesting or giving thanks for the healing of babies; totally understandable, given the high mortality rates. A popular votive offering was a wax candle. It may not seem much to us today, but in medieval times wax was expensive and only wealthy people could afford them. Such a gift was considered very special and the cathedral, because of its value, would burn them. Hence, very few of these gifts have survived. Another gift affordable by most people was that of a 'bent penny'. A penny would be deliberately bent in half, used as a prayer votive and then left as a gift for the saint.

As always, the Reformation sought, by vandalism and massive destruction of church fabric, to eliminate idolatry and corruption.

Thomas's original shrine was placed in the north transept, but he was translated* to a new shrine in the Lady Chapel. This was elaborate with a heavily decorated reliquary and a colourful canopy. The Protestant reformers smashed this shrine to pieces and nothing remained of either Thomas's relics or his shrine, and his bones were never found. By pure luck, however, his original tomb and shrine in the transept had never been moved, and remained in situ. The vandals, not knowing about it, left it intact, and it is at this shrine that people venerate St Thomas today. A table shrine, it is decorated on its sides with carvings of knights in armour in various stances and garbs. Originally, these would have been highly coloured and must have been beautiful to see. Chairs for quiet prayer and meditation are placed close by; a tranquil spot to remember Hereford's second saint.

Before leaving Symonds Yat next day, despite miserable, damp weather and heavy mist we decided we would still like to go to the top of the rock. We cheated, however, because instead of making a steep climb we drove up, as most do, to a car park near to the viewing area. And it was indeed a splendid sight. Even on such a day there were a lot of people, and we could understand why. Of course, the view was not at its best, but we could still see far down the meandering River Wye, which here takes a massive curve around the rock, making the rock seem almost like an island. One thing we didn't see: the peregrine falcons, for which the Yat is well known. In the summer impressive numbers can be seen soaring high above the gorge, circling, searching for food to take back to the nests where they breed on the inaccessible and perfect terrain.

On the road between Hereford and Symonds Yat, we had on a number of occasions passed a hotel called The Pilgrim. Of course I couldn't not visit, and after our walk in rain and mist we thought it a perfect excuse to call in there for a warming whisky. We were pleased too to find a choice of a few nice single malts, of which Malc and I are rather partial. I spoke to the manager and asked what was the link with pilgrims. Disappointingly, there was none, but the owner liked the history around. The road on which the hotel stood was the main pilgrim route from Swansea in South

* Meaning 'moved'.

Wales to Hereford. That was a good enough reason for me.

We set off for home carrying with us a message for a friend in Carlisle. Before we left the cathedral I spoke with an officer who was tidying seats. He was Stephen, one of four vergers who work at the cathedral.

"Have you a bit of a problem?" I asked him as he continued to rehang and rearrange the kneelers in the pews.

"The youngsters from the cathedral school use this area when they come over for worship. They manage to somehow get things a bit disordered." He smiled.

During further conversation, he asked where we had come from.

We told him, "North of the Border, but we worship at Carlisle Cathedral."

"Oh, do you? Well, do say hello to James for me."

James is a verger at Carlisle. It does seem a small world! But then, with only a small number of cathedral vergers, it isn't really surprising they all know each other. When on our next visit to Carlisle, James was equally surprised to receive verger Stephen's good wishes from a colleague down in Herefordshire, but it was nice to tell him of our encounter.

Our final memory of Hereford as we prepared to set off for home was seeing a lovely scallop shell carved into the stone in front of the cathedral entrance. This sign of the pilgrim was a lovely image to remind us.

Pilgrim shell symbol, Hereford Cathedral.

Middle Ages pilgrims.

Large mistletoe bough in full leaf and covered in berries.

Leafless trees, with boughs of hanging mistletoe in and around Hereford.

Shrine of St Thomas de Cantilupe, Hereford Cathedral.

kagyu Samye Ling

AN UNEXPECTED JEWEL: SAMYE LING

Malc and I were travelling along a prehistoric trail in the north-east of Dumfries and Galloway. Although classed as Lowland Scotland, this area is nevertheless one of high hills, forest, bracken, sheep and few people. There are also a remarkable number of prehistoric sites, stone circles, hill forts, mysterious amphitheatres, and also Roman forts, their outlines under the earth showing clearly on the hillsides. This is a beautiful and empty landscape and was possibly more heavily populated in prehistory than it is today. The trail lies between two rivers, the White and Black Esk, which combine further along the valley to become just the River Esk. Named after this lovely salmon river, we are in Eskdale. The road undulates, but we finally come down into the valley and into the village of Eskdalemuir, a small, isolated village several miles from a town. On a late autumn day we had enjoyed our drive.

"It's beautiful, Malc," I said.

Not having been in this area for a while, I had forgotten how spectacular and quiet it was. The colours were stunning, bracken russet on the hillsides and the stands of forest with a range of evergreen and deciduous trees lent a tapestry of colour from purple through green to red and gold. It was calm, cold and crisp, a perfect autumn day. Even if there was nothing else of interest, this area already seemed complete, and yet just a mile further on from the village stands an amazing and quite unforgettable sight. If not expecting it, travellers would see something extraordinary and think maybe they had had a couple of drinks too many. They would stop and go back to check. But no, their minds are not playing tricks. The flamboyant golden-roofed buildings, cupolas and floating golden statues are real, for this is Samye Ling Buddhist Monastery and Tibetan Centre. It truly is an unexpected site, incongruous in the Scottish landscape, but vibrant, visually striking and totally other-worldly. Although continuing to expand, the monastery has actually been here since 1967. It is now a well-rooted fixture, but puzzled visitors still say, "Why here, in the wilds and remoteness of South-West Scotland?" The strangeness is more confounding when realising that in 1967, and for many years after, this was the first and only Buddhist centre to emerge from Tibet into the West. It flourishes here, and the two elements of monastery and visitor centre bring many people to see it and others to live and learn here. Once in the grounds, it is as if you have been transported back to Tibet. It is a visual and sensory experience that is hard to beat.

The focus is the temple, which is used daily and welcomes any visitors who are quiet and prepared to take off their shoes. Although outwardly not unprepossessing, it is inside the temple where your senses are stretched to the limit. The colours are vibrant golds and reds, and there is the smell of incense. The walls are covered with cabinets full of scrolls and Buddha statues. There is an altar, but no pews. Prayer is made from mats and cushions on the floor. Just looking around, you are aware that this is something well out of your experience, but its atmosphere is calm and welcoming.

The grounds are equally spectacular, with garden areas, statues, lakes and a traditional 'stupa' garden, where a circular path is laid. This path is walked in an anticlockwise direction. In this stupa garden, Scottish and Tibetan traditions meet in the form of a 'cloutie tree'. The tree is covered in thousands of pieces of cloth, each one tied to a branch. When tying the cloth, a prayer is said, and this stays with the tree until such time as the wind blows the prayer away or the colour of the cloth fades with time, the disappearing colour taking the prayer with it. Only once the prayer has flown will its request be considered. Cloutie is a Scottish word meaning cloth and the word is used in the name of the Scottish dish of cloutie dumpling, a fruit pudding made with suet, which is steamed for many hours in the hope it is worth the time, money and effort that went into making it! When I tried it, the finished result looked anything but appetising and it didn't taste any better than it looked, but I am no great cook!

Samye Ling is named after the first monastery in Tibet and follows the Tibetan and tantric form, which was first established in the fifth century AD. There are many branches of Buddhism and, whilst all have core elements, there are also many differences between each branch. Most of us not familiar with the Buddhist faith probably associate Buddhism with lamas, and the Dalai Lama in particular. Yet it is only the Tibetan branch which has lamas.

Wanting to find out a little more about how Samye Ling functions, I spoke to Michael, who was at the time acting as receptionist. Michael is a volunteer and lives on-site, but supports himself.

"At any one time," he said, "there are resident monks and nuns; at present there are eight monks and eight nuns."

He told us they come not only from the UK, but from across the world. Whereas, however, Christian monks and nuns enter a religious house where they mostly remain for life, this is not the case with Buddhism, where they may stay for short periods in many different places. At Samye Ling the complement changes as people come and go to complete and extend their training. It is therefore described as a 'teaching' monastery.

In charge of the monastery is a lama, Choje Lama, Yeshe Losal Rinpoche. He replaced his brother, Choje Akong Tulku Rinpoche, who was the original founder here. Tragically, he was murdered on a visit to China in 2013. A memorial to him has been established here, with an exhibition of his life and work.

I was surprised to learn from Michael that the centre, in its more public areas, is more or less run by volunteers. Indeed, the impressive temple was built entirely by volunteers and opened in 1988. Michael said there were currently around twelve volunteers, and I was astounded at what seemed a small number considering the amount of work needed to run this large place.

"It is hard!" he replied.

There are offices, a retreat centre, guest houses and teaching courses to be maintained, as well as a café and shop. I asked if he had a religious role.

"No," he replied, "I am purely a volunteer, but I believe in the Buddhist faith and attend the temple and prayers when I can."

"Have you not considered moving on to become a monk?"

He smiled. "No, not really. It is very, very difficult."

I could understand that because I was finding it very hard to truly understand the spirit and faith of Buddhism.

All Buddhists relate to the original Buddha, Prince Siddartha, who after many years of personal sacrifice, wanderings and meditation believed he had found the way to the ultimate meaning of life. He reached a state of enlightenment and nirvana, and by following his guidance all followers could, he said, achieve the same. Though not everyone can reach this elevated state, everyone can nevertheless progress through to improve their life and their next life.

He prescribes followers to undertake the noble eightfold path, not a consecutive path of different levels, but all eight to be undertaken at the same time. These eight rules all begin with 'right', followed by understanding, thought, speech, conduct, occupation, effort, mindfulness and concentration. This comprises the Buddhist law.

Although it is a religion, Buddhism does not have a god. Buddha is a respected and revered leader, to whom Buddhists pray. They aspire to follow his teachings, but he is not worshipped as an all-encompassing god. It is complex, and I gathered from Michael that there are many levels of spiritual revelation and it takes many years to learn and understand.

Refreshments were calling, so we visited the Tibetan Tea Rooms. The River Esk runs alongside the centre and lovely walks along its banks are an extra attraction here. In summer the whole complex can be very busy, but in late autumn it was peaceful, the garden areas empty and the river path soothing as we watched the river flowing by.

In the tea rooms I spoke to Nina, another volunteer, this day running the café. As befits the international flavour of Samye Ling, Nina was from Holland, where she had been a successful fine artist for many years before coming to Samye Ling about a year ago.

"What brought you here?" I asked her.

This proved a difficult question for her to answer, and I imagine this is the same for many of the volunteers here. She did try to explain though.

"I was already familiar with meditation when I was in Holland, where I had a Zen teacher. Somehow I needed to refocus my life away from the mainstream of society."

It was through other people that she heard of Samye Ling and she eventually came to live here.

"And have you managed to find yourself?" I asked, perhaps rather too glibly.

"No," she replied, "just the opposite."

She is at a crossroads in her life, taking advice, meditating and being taught at the centre, sometimes even by the lama himself. But she is unsure what she will do in the future.

"It is really hard," she emphasised.

I appreciated Nina speaking to me and I wished her well. She was a genuine person, searching, as we often all are at certain parts of our lives. I really hope she finds what she is seeking.

Feeling refreshed and conscious of the short autumn days, Malc and I decided to take a last look around. A new building had been added fairly recently, a place to house prayer wheels, which are also in evidence in the temple. These prayer wheels are a feature of the Tibetan Buddhist branch, and their purpose is very similar to that of the cloutie tree. Inside each large wheel, which is in perpetual motion, are millions of prayers, released into the atmosphere by movement. Prayer flags around the centre have the same purpose and are very much part of the Tibetan tradition.

Pilgrimage does not seem to be a key feature of Buddhism, although festivals celebrating the Buddha are popular. Also what does pilgrimage mean? Certainly people come to Samye Ling for many reasons – for learning, curiosity and enlightenment. There is also a popular tradition of retreat, which is probably an aid to meditation. Volunteer Michael and I had a little discussion about this, Michael stressing that the meaning of retreat is very fluid. Whereas I and other Christians might attend a day or several days on a retreat, at Samye Ling, I learned, people enter a retreat for several months. Pilgrimage is not an uppermost activity. The Temple of the Tooth in Sri Lanka is said to hold a tooth of Buddha and is a popular pilgrimage centre, but they are rare.

In the end I decided that Samye Ling is hard to define in respect of pilgrimage. It does not have saints, healing wells or relics, but it is a place of spiritual enlightenment, a focus for people to look at their spiritual life and to encourage thought. It doesn't match the other types of pilgrim places, but then it is so different I am not sure it could. What it offers is a valuable experience, even if difficult for people like me to really understand. In the end it doesn't matter. People seek out a place of spiritual enrichment, and maybe this search is in itself a pilgrimage.

Samye Ling means 'place beyond imagination'. It certainly is such. From the saffron-clad monks and nuns with their shaven heads seen wandering around Lockerbie and Langholm* doing necessary shopping, to the golden, awe-inspiring buildings, to the prayer wheels and incense, it remains to me a place of mystery, of somewhere beyond Scotland in a landscape of snow and mountains far away in a distant land.

* Langholm is another local town on the Esk.

Both photos are of loating statues in the Stupa Garden.

The blind shall see if they
come to the shrine.
The cripple who comes limping
is healed.
If someone brings here a
madman, he will leave
with a sound mind.

A WINTER PILGRIMAGE:
ST WINIFREDE AT HOLYWELL

"Oh no, Malc!" I exclaimed, "it's closed."

"It can't be," came the reply, "it's open all year."

"It may say that, and the information board here confirms it, but there is a padlocked gate right in front of me and a large sign which says 'Closed', so I rather think it is."

"It's ridiculous!" Malc continued. "Is there no explanation? I can't believe we have come all this way from Scotland and it's closed."

"Well, it is."

Admittedly, it was a bitterly cold day with crisp snow underfoot and snow flurries silently gliding down, wetting us as we stood in the open, wondering what to do. Even so, it should have been open.

We were in North Wales in the small town of Holywell, named after the well associated here with St Winifrede. Its healing properties and the legacy of Winifrede made this place a popular pilgrim site, and it has remained in continual use for over 1,400 years (except the day we visited). People came to bathe in its waters, or to be sprinkled, and then to pray in the pilgrim church, which spans the well. Considered to be one of the finest surviving examples of a medieval holy well in Britain, the church too is a scheduled ancient monument and is grade-A listed. Built in the sixteenth century, it is regarded as a beautiful and sophisticated example and recognised gem of Perpendicular architecture, unique in the world. And we couldn't get into this either! We thought we might be able to find the custodian, whose house was on-site, but heavy knocking was to no avail. The place was totally deserted. We wandered around the periphery of the site and took some photographs at a distance from behind the surrounding walls, but we were so disappointed and frustrated. There seemed no alternative but to go back to the car, to warm up if nothing else, and consider our options if there were any.

I remembered that there is a guest house which caters specially for pilgrims to the well. Could they help us? we wondered. It was only a short walk uphill, where we saw a beautiful large Georgian house, one of many buildings in the area which have catered for pilgrims over hundreds of years. This was the most recent. Unfortunately it too looked deserted, but we knocked anyway! Just as we were about to walk away the door opened and we were met by an elderly nun in a colourful apron who was either cooking lunch or was clearing away. She invited us in out of the cold and was kind and as helpful as possible, yet couldn't really solve our problem. She didn't know why it was closed.

"What about the custodian?" I asked her. "We knocked, but there was no answer."

"No," she replied, "there is a new custodian now who no longer lives on-site."

There was nothing more we could do, but whilst there I asked her about the guest house. It is actually a convent for nuns run by the Catholic Church, and it also offers accommodation to pilgrims.

"I'm so sorry to disturb you," I said when I realised it was a convent, unsure whether she was supposed to talk with me, but she reassured me it was fine. "So how many nuns do you have here?"

"There used to be seven of us, but now there are only four."

I felt sorry on several accounts, that the monastic heritage of hospitality here seemed to be struggling, and it would only get harder as the nuns grow older. We thanked her and headed back to our car, still disappointed at our fruitless journey. Yes, we could see the well over the walls, but I had really wanted to sprinkle the healing water over me, recognising it was rather stupid to expect to bathe unless I wanted to experience frostbite. So does the water have special powers?

But we had at least seen the guest house, a really important element of pilgrim support over many centuries.

What is now a convent and guest house was originally a hospice. In pilgrimage terms this had a very different meaning than it does today, the tradition stretching right back into history. Hospices were first established in the eleventh century, during the Crusades, for the benefit of pilgrims to the Holy Land. This was an extremely popular thing to do, but involved a long, difficult and expensive journey. It was also dangerous. As well as the possibility of becoming involved in the fighting between Christians and Muslims, there was also a very real possibility of being attacked and robbed. Knightly orders, such as the Templars and the Knights of St John, were charged by the English king with the responsibility of making pilgrim routes safer and less arduous. These knightly orders grew in numbers, influence and wealth and were able to establish safe routes, including watchers along the routes, as well as setting up refuges at certain points along the way. There pilgrims could rest and stay in safety and they could also find food and accommodation. Over time, these refuges became more specialised, becoming hospices for sick and disabled pilgrims and guest houses for the more able-bodied. Many religious houses took on this role, becoming well known for hospitality not just in the Holy Land, but across Europe, in particular in places along pilgrim routes. The knights raised money for these wayside safe houses and, as time went by, hospitality was given free to pilgrims in recognition of the respect in which they were held.

It became an expected norm during the early Middle Ages that people should, where possible, offer support, help and hospitality to all genuine pilgrims. Assurance that pilgrims were genuine was often in the form of a pilgrim badge, and most shrines would have their own unique badge, recognised as authentic. The ubiquitous scallop-shell badge was known through Europe and the Middle East as a true pilgrim symbol. The tradition of hospitality grew and continued until the Reformation and the destruction of so many religious houses.

Those remaining today, such as the one at Holywell, bear testament to this ancient tradition of supporting pilgrims. In North

Wales the first hospice assisting those who were sick and disabled, and who had come seeking healing, was provided by monks at Basingwerk, a little inland from Holywell. The service continued until 1537 and the Reformation. After a 100-year gap, the Jesuit movement attempted to recreate a facility, this time in the town of Holywell itself. An inn, The Star, was made available, and from the mid 1600s a form of accommodation has continued offering a vital service for sick and dying pilgrims. The service was not completely free, however, though it was subsidised and cheap. In 1870 it cost three shillings and sixpence for a week's full board, whilst in 1939 it was charged at a daily rate of two shillings. Pilgrim numbers varied over the years, but never completely dried up. The total numbers of pilgrims are unknown, but the hospice itself kept records. In 1892, 284 people were admitted, predominantly women. Many were said to be pitifully sick and needed help to access the healing water. The year 1895 saw more pilgrims when 1,710 stayed at the hospice, 500 of whom were sick. Many brought companions.

Of course, times have changed, but accommodation is still provided here by the few nuns up the hill in the guest house, fulfilling the same purpose as it did over 1,000 years ago.

Before leaving the well site we read an information board at the side of the road. Here was written a verse of encouragement for pilgrims from many years ago:

The blind shall see if they
come to the shrine.
The cripple who comes limping
is healed.
If someone brings here a
madman, he will leave
with a sound mind.

These words make some astounding claims, the result of fanciful faith, or known results?

We decided to head back to Chester, where we were staying, only a few miles over the border in Cheshire, and I suggested we took the coast road back. The area closest to Holywell is the Dee Estuary, a beautiful area of estuarial salt flats, marsh and sandbanks, a perfect place for thousands of overwintering seabirds in the rich feeding area where the Dee flows in and out of Chester, once an important port. Across the estuary, the Wirral Peninsula in England provides a picturesque backdrop. At the same time this area of North Wales forms part of a huge heavy-industrial belt reaching into Merseyside and Cheshire. Shotton Steelworks is here, once a major manufacturer and employer of hundreds of people, its industrial might, however, now sadly depleted.

Following the coast road, the coast itself was obscured by modern equivalents with mile upon mile of retail parks, offices and business parks. We knew there was a lovely coast somewhere here, but it was hard to find.

One coastal landmark, however, was hard to miss. The *Duke of Lancaster*, a former ferry, is now a huge beached wreck of a boat. Well, perhaps 'wreck' is too strong a word, but abandoned it certainly is. Originally brought here as a commercial enterprise, its new owner intended it as a fun ship, with a restaurant and nightclub. This never materialised. With 'fun' removed, it is now just a ship – a rusting hulk, a focal point on the coast, incongruous as it is. But whilst we could see it from the road, we couldn't find a way down to it!

Eventually, after parking the car we walked about and found a footpath which not only took us to the ship, but to the coastal path too. This path runs from Queensferry on the Welsh border to Prestatyn and the tourist coast around Rhyl and Colwyn Bay. Once away from the heavily urbanised areas, it provided a lovely walk with expansive views across the estuary to England.

Industry is nothing new to this area. An information board told us that manufacturing here goes right back to Roman times, when lead was brought here for smelting. Later, the waters of the Dee Estuary proved perfect for boats, and small ports and docks developed. You can still see evidence of these, with remains of wooden jetties slowly rotting, bearing testament to these earlier times. One of these small docks was at Greenfield, and this was where pilgrims coming to St Winifrede's Well would disembark and then continue the rest of the short way through fields on foot.

Winifrede was a woman of the Dark Ages, born sometime in the seventh century AD and dying in 660. Like so many early saints, it is hard to separate out in her story the parts which are true from those which are apocryphal or even legend. She was apparently born in Flintshire in the place known as Holywell today and was the daughter of a noble family, one which had a history of saintly and monastic members. It was no surprise when she expressed her wish to become a nun. She did, in fact, also have a suitor, believed to be called Caradog, a man of high status and noble blood. He was none too pleased when his future bride decided instead to become a nun. He was incensed that she would spurn him and he became so angry that he reputedly decapitated her. The story continues with her uncle, who was St Beuno, who picked up her head and miraculously reattached it so that she lived and took up her vocation in a nearby nunnery. Her spurned lover was supposedly killed. Where her head had fallen a spring emerged, and this spring flowed, becoming Winifrede's healing well! Now, I believe in miracles, and I believe in alternative types of healing and spiritual healing, but this story does somehow seem, shall we say, a little far-fetched.

Nevertheless, there do seem to be some discernible even authentic facts. There is some evidence that Winifrede did exist at this time, and although she was not decapitated she was severely wounded. An ancient document recounts that after the attack she had for the rest of her life a large scar around her neck. We know too that her uncle, Beuno, did exist as well. He was St Beuno and, whatever happened, he appears to have saved her life, the spring emerging representing the fact she was saved for a reason and that her uncle being present was purposeful, not just providential.

At Nefyn in Gwynedd there is a St Beuno's Chapel, and he is reputed to be buried under the altar. The chapel is famous for its annual celebration of Lammas Day – an ancient festival celebrating the first harvesting in August. The church is decorated on this day with tokens of harvest sheaves of wheat and other representations. This chapel was also on the pilgrim route from Holywell to Bardsey, an island off the Welsh coast and another highly venerated pilgrim site. The chapel served as a halt, where pilgrims could rest from their journey before continuing to Bardsey. As early as the twelfth century this pilgrim route was already well established.

Winifrede spent the rest of her life at a nunnery in what is now Denbighshire, becoming abbess, and was respected and revered as a very holy devout woman of God.

But it was the well which became the source of healing, not Winifrede herself. As a result, it is interesting that because of this she was never formally canonised by the Catholic Church, but was accredited with sainthood because of many centuries of veneration. She was given 3 November as her saint's day.

Her reputation even in her lifetime spread, and a swell of affection and conviction in the powers of the healing well brought pilgrims from a distance, as well as local, evidenced by the boat journeys.

Later analysis of the water showed that it had some unusual qualities. Within it were two distinct and unusual algae which were found to have healing qualities and were also good and nutritious to eat.

Her fame spread, and sometime after her death, when she had been buried at her own abbey, she was exhumed and translated to Shrewsbury Abbey, where her relics were venerated for many centuries. But that is another story.

Of course, water had a special place in people's lives for many centuries, since well before the Christian era. Many religious and social practices have been associated with water. Today in Derbyshire the annual well-dressing ceremonies at village wells across the county are many centuries old. Water, wells, lakes and bogs, held mystery and superstition. They could hold magic powers and were the dwelling places of spirits and fairies, and of course pure, clean water is vital for life. It has always been venerated and protected. This tradition clearly held sway elsewhere. Jesus was baptised in the River Jordan, for commitment, purification and belief. So to the people of the Dark and Middle Ages water was still an element of mystery and healing. Many illnesses were incurable and also frightening, and the potentially healing waters blessed by spiritual leaders and saints provided a popular way to seek healing. Pilgrimage provided an opportunity to seek out these places, even if the journey was long, difficult and expensive. Even the development of greater and more sophisticated knowledge did not deter these beliefs. In the seventeenth and eighteenth centuries spa towns became the place to be. Towns such as Bath, Buxton and Leamington Spa flourished as the disabled and wealthy people descended to take the waters, and also to be seen. Of course, even now we know that different spring or spa waters are very individual and possess certain elements which may have health benefits.

The coast road led us back to Chester and our hotel. This is a city which quite understandably attracts visitors of all nationalities. It seems to have everything: Roman remains in abundance, a beautiful river and meadows, double-height seventeenth-century shopping arcades, an old and beautiful cathedral and encircling town walls. Yet I became fascinated by something else entirely, much less dramatic and possibly even insignificant.

Our hotel room fronted on to a city-centre street, and throughout the night we became intrigued by continual flashing lights. They turned out to be Belisha beacons, the forerunner of modern-day pelican crossings with the usual wait and cross lights. The Belisha beacons consisted of a bright flashing amber globe on top of a black-and-white pole situated on the kerb on either side of a crossing. They were invented in 1937 by Lord Hore Belisha and they were in use for many decades. I can just remember them, but I was surprised that any survived, let alone still in regular use. Yet these old-fashioned crossings seemed to still work remarkably well, even in today's traffic-saturated cities. We watched people trudging to work in the morning's snowfall, and everyone seemed to use these crossings, of which there were three directly below our bedroom window. Motorists continually stopped to give way to pedestrians, an old-fashioned remnant of when crossings were based on driver courtesy and kindness rather than traffic-light enforcement. Even in the midst of the busy morning rush hour this simple system seemed to work.

My first failed pilgrimage was disappointing, but we enjoyed our trip nonetheless. It gave me the opportunity to visit an old friend and colleague. When I had to retire on grounds of ill health, he went on to greater things as chief executive of Chester Council. Whilst Chester's heritage is the attraction for visitors, ensuring its protection and enhancement is crucial for the economy of the city. But it is also a living, breathing modern city and its thousands of residents have needs which the council needs to address. Of course, towns have always changed and developed, responding to changing times, and one building in the heart of the city is a perfect example of how to turn round a failing building. At a cost of £37 million it was a project which needed to succeed. My friend quite rightly wanted me to see it.

The former Odeon cinema is a massive edifice of beautiful art deco architecture, but as a cinema it was redundant and had long stood empty and sad. Under the transformation it is now the Storyhouse. Ideas for its new use needed to be forward-thinking and impressive, yet retaining its character and beauty. There is now a cinema again, but the building now also incorporates two theatres with a repertory company; a new 'old' idea. What I found particularly innovative is that the walls all around the entire building are lined with books. For here too is the revamped city library. Across the country libraries are failing, being closed or drastically reduced in size. In the Storyhouse it was decided not to retain the library as a separate entity, but to relocate it here and incorporate it within the building as a whole. There are large informal seating areas, comfortable and colourful with electric-blue, teal, red, green and gold velvet-covered chairs, reflecting the colours of the art deco period. It has an opulent and luxurious yet welcoming feel. When Malc and I visited there was a mixture of people relaxing here, couples, mums with toddlers, students and retirees, or browsing through the books, papers and magazines, which was precisely the intention. One of the largest areas is adjacent to the café, so a read, relaxation and a cup of tea were a nice combination. This new café also serves relatively cheap food with a deliberately different and changing menu. No paninis here – yay!

So far everything seems to be working harmoniously. Book lending has increased significantly and the theatre productions, despite fairly high ticket prices, are well attended. During our tour we were shown the booking screen for the next production, a musical, which was already ninety per cent booked. No wonder the Storyhouse has become a flagship which other towns are keen to emulate.

Overall, it had been a funny sort of trip, with hiccups and disappointments, but also unexpected highlights. Now it was time to go home.

Our journey down had been eventful, finding a traffic tailback on the M6 at Warrington of one and half hours! We knew the area, so by looking at the map we managed to divert across Merseyside, crossing the River Mersey by the new bridge at Runcorn and continuing on to the Chester road. We hoped our return journey would be more straightforward. However, there was snow across the country, which was proving hazardous, and we were apprehensive, tense, but then pleased when all the way up, the M6 motorway was clear. Everywhere was snowy, the Lake District a complete white-out, so beautiful, the jagged hilltops smoothed out by snowfall. But the beauty was superseded by our anxiety to get home safely before dark. It was on reaching Gretna Green that conditions really started to deteriorate, with only one lane open and that was snowy too. After another few miles we came to our turn-off and we both heaved a site of relief.

"We are home safely," I said. "Thank goodness!"

Little did we know that in fact this was the start of our problems. From the motorway the road climbs steadily to our village. Cars had clearly never moved all day, enveloped in snow. There was just no one about and it was dark and eerily quiet. At the first major incline we knew we were not going to make it as the car wheels spun and we slithered about the road in all directions. No gritters seemed to have been and snowploughs hadn't reached us. There was no alternative but to abandon the car, which had fortunately slithered down almost to the roadside. We both sat in the car, neither at first saying anything, my mind had gone completely blank.

Then, almost simultaneously, we both said, "So what do we do now?"

A pause and I said, "Perhaps we can walk?"

"You must be joking!" Malcolm replied, flabbergasted. "The snow is more than knee-deep, it's three miles uphill and it's at least minus five."

End of suggestion. Quiet again.

"Mm, see what you mean!" I agreed.

Then a miracle happened. Was it the belated miracle we didn't get at St Winifrede's Well? It seemed like it at the time. Behind the car we saw some lights – moving lights – approaching us on the road. It was a tractor, and as it drew closer Malc flashed the car lights and it stopped. It was actually our neighbour, the farmer from just behind our house. What luck! I grabbed my coat and handbag; Malc came just as he was and abandoned everything else in the car and the car itself. We squeezed into the tractor cab with James, his girlfriend and Flo the sheepdog. It was all very cosy. I didn't care. I would have sat on the roof if it meant I could get home. It was the first time either of us had been rescued by a tractor, and how grateful we were!

I have never felt so good to be home. What an end to our journey! We may not have been able to get into St Winifrede's Well, but I don't think I will risk going back. Two days later we were still snowed in and our car was still abandoned at the roadside!

Holywell, North Wales, on a very, very cold and snowy day. This shows the church which spans the well of St Winifrede.

St Winifrede's Well, with steep steps for descending in order to bathe and immerse in the 'healing' water.

The Duke of Lancaster, *a former ferry now abandoned and beached on the Holywell coast.*

A TRANSLATED SAINT:
ST WINIFREDE'S TRIP TO SHREWSBURY

The demand for relics by monastic houses, abbeys and cathedrals in the early Middle Ages was so great that they were sought from all quarters. Procuring the body, clothes or belongings of a saint promised great wealth to these religious establishments. Pilgrims, ever eager to travel to a shrine, would contribute to the town economy; and by gifts and donations, as well as by the purchase of souvenirs, the Church accrued great wealth and prestige.

Every church of any importance wanted its relics. To this end, it was not uncommon for relics to be 'found' (probably stolen) or removed for safekeeping (an excuse). They would then be translated (relocated) to a new home, where they would be placed in a tomb, shrine, reliquary or all three, mostly made of stone. Then the religious house would wait, first for a trickle and then, hopefully, a torrent of pilgrims.

This is precisely what happened at Shrewsbury. We first encountered Winifrede in North Wales, where her well is still attracting pilgrims. When she died she was buried at Gwytherin in Flintshire, where she had lived at the convent. Where money could be made, however, saints could not guarantee that their mortal remains would remain at peace in their chosen burial spot. So it was that in 1138 a Shrewsbury abbot carried her bones wrapped in linen to Shrewsbury, where she was translated and reinterred. Winifrede had been recognised as a healer, as a result of her well, but in Shrewsbury it would seem that her bones were now seen as relics which could heal. Pilgrims made their way to Shrewsbury Abbey, believers in her power.

Shrewsbury Abbey Church in Shropshire is a wonderful but also sad reminder of all that was lost when Henry VIII began his purge of religious buildings in 1536. So much was lost – beautiful architecture, artefacts, art – and a way of life was almost eradicated. Some places escaped desecration purely by chance, and it is remarkable that we can still appreciate such treasures.

Shrewsbury Abbey Church survived only because at the time the public of the town were allowed to worship here. Thus it was saved and allowed to become a parish church. Apart from a few stones, the church is the sole survivor of the Abbey of St Peter and St Paul. Its fortunes suffered further over time.

When Malc and I visited it was a cold, damp, drab, misty day in November. It was drizzling too, the kind you can't see, but which wets you through within minutes. We found the abbey church easily enough, but it was a surprise to find it sort of wedged into a triangle of land surrounded by roads (on both sides) with heavy traffic, a railway and a canal, as well as being close to shops and pubs. In its heyday in the early Middle Ages, the abbey would have been set slightly apart from the town, not surrounded by it. Up until the mid nineteenth century more of the abbey had survived, but when the famous Thomas Telford, who was the town surveyor, altered the road system, he ploughed right through the abbey precinct. Today that road still passes right by the church and onward straight into town. Despite a few remaining fragments, to all intents and purposes we are now left with just a church. But what a church! It may not be the grandest, but it has a simplicity of style, rendering it stocky and sturdy. It seems to shout out, however, saying, "Look at me – I'm still here!"

This abbey is most popularly known from the books by Ellis Peters. Her main character, the monk Cadfael, lives in the abbey here, and, as well as being a herbalist, he cleverly solves many murders and other crimes, which unfortunately seem to have proliferated in the eleventh century. Hopefully the real Shrewsbury at that time was much less violent! Much of the background to her books is authentic, and as a beloved fictional character he is very popular. Visitors can now take a 'Cadfael Trail' around the city.

My purpose, however, was to trace the story of a real person, St Winifrede of Holywell. As I have discovered in so many of these shrine places, only scant remains have endured. From what is believed to have been an impressive stone shrine, beautifully carved, only a fragment now survives: a small stone slab, probably the side of the shrine, which still shows three figures carved into the stone. These carvings are believed to be of St Winifrede, St Beuno and John the Baptist. Beuno was Winifrede's uncle and we met him at Holywell. He was the person who saved her life after she was decapitated by her spurned lover. St Beuno seems to be a recognised person, and a church named after him exists at Nefyn (Pistyll), Gwynedd. This church sits on the route to Bardsey Island, off the Welsh coast, another important early twelfth-century pilgrim site, where travelling pilgrims would halt at this chapel. Today it is known as a church which celebrates Lammas Day – an ancient festival recognising the first harvest days. Decorated with wheat and other cereal stalks, haystacks, wool and other harvest images, it is one of a few churches celebrating this particular festival. Pilgrims thronged to the shrine of St Winifrede, in Shrewsbury some on a longer journey covering a number of pilgrim sites, others perhaps finding time to visit just this one. There is one other remaining fragment, in the abbey a seal of Winifrede. The engraving on this seal shows her kneeling on the ground, her attacker holding a sword high, about to decapitate her.

Today a lovely window with many symbols relevant to Winifrede and Wales stands above the shrine. Little else remains to remind us of a Welsh saint who drew many pilgrims to Shrewsbury Abbey. It would once have been a busy, exciting place, with hopes and expectations high as the pilgrims prayed to her. Today we can only use our imagination of how it would have looked in the early first-millennium years.

Of course, unlike today, there would then also have been the whole abbey complex, comprising living quarters for many monks and guest houses and refectories for pilgrims. Hopefully some would be going home healed and fortified and in a better physical and spiritual state than when they arrived. Pilgrims could share their experiences, emotions and excitement high, enjoying visiting a different place and sharing news with friends and other travellers.

When Malc and I first entered the abbey church we felt a distinct atmosphere. It did feel old (and of course it is), but also seemed to display and communicate its difficult survival. It was as if it had its war wounds, strange words, I admit, but I felt much the same when I went to Hexham Abbey. Buildings do have atmospheres, both good and bad, reassuring or scary. This was not any of these, but it did speak to us of all those centuries and what it must have seen.

There was nothing commercial about this church, and I imagine few now come, like me, as a pilgrim. And indeed it truly has suffered many different crises.

As the county town of Shropshire, Shrewsbury is an old town which retains its medieval heart, but which has also suffered from centuries of battles and skirmishes resulting from its close proximity to the Welsh border. It also sits on the banks of the lovely River Severn. However, this is not a lovely river when it floods, as it often does, and on at least three occasions these floods have caused devastation to the town. Photographs inside the abbey show the last major flood, where the water was so deep that boats were sailing down the church aisles.

Yet this church is not a church of the past. Its history, destruction and miraculous survival has brought it into the twenty-first century, where it does not just survive, indeed, it is flourishing.

Scattered around the church are several very impressive tombs, elaborate and decorative, which also retain evidence of paintwork in various bright colours. Whole monuments would originally have been brightly painted, striking and impressive as of course they were meant to be. Winifrede's shrine may also have been coloured, and pilgrims would have appreciated the beauty and craftsmanship, all enhancing the pilgrim experience.

This would also encourage pilgrims and give confidence and optimism in the power of the saint. They knew they were in the presence of a wonderful, important and worthy saint. They would have felt very confident of the power of the saint lying within the shrine.

As a person of the more enlightened twenty-first century, I am naturally sceptical about Winifrede, and the story of how after decapitation her head was replaced and brought back to life. Yet in the Middle Ages such were people's faith and acceptance that they would not for a moment have doubted the idea of a miracle such as that experienced by Winifrede. To them it proved that God is indeed miraculous, worthy of praise, worship and total belief in His powers. Such things were an encouragement to them, demonstrating God's power, and here a pilgrim could seek His presence and power exerted through His saints. Yes, pilgrims were gullible. They were exploited, but no one can deny that purportedly people did come away from the shrine, if not healed, then uplifted and joyful.

The seal of St Winifrede, showing her being decapitated, in Shrewsbury abbey.

A RARITY IN THE PEAKS:
ST BERTRAM, DOVEDALE

Bertram is another saint from late Saxon times, but he lived in the Midlands. Reputed to be a member of the Mercian royal family, this old Saxon kingdom of Mercia comprised much of Central England. Legend tells us that Bertram eloped with an Irish princess and then, wishing to return home, he journeyed with his now pregnant wife. Before reaching the safety of home, his wife went into labour. Bertram desperately sought a midwife, but by the time he returned his wife had given birth, and both she and her baby were dead. It appeared they had been killed and savaged by wolves. Anguished, full of guilt about travelling with his wife at such a difficult time, and remorseful, thinking he was responsible, Bertram never recovered from their deaths. For the rest of his life he was a recluse, becoming a revered holy man. People heard of him and sought his counsel, believing his experiences and insights had made him wise. Later too he was found to have powers of healing, and it was evidence of these healing miracles which led to his being made a saint. Bertram lived the rest of his life in prayer and meditation, some of the time in a cave which can still be seen. In this way he was able to atone for his guilt. He lived his life in the village of Ilam in Staffordshire, in what today is the Peak District, the first national park to be established in the UK.

We mostly think of the Peak District as being in Derbyshire, but some, as at Ilam, is in the equally lovely Staffordshire Moorlands.

Ilam is in the valley of the River Manifold, but we were staying over the county line, just a couple of miles away in Dovedale, Derbyshire. This is possibly the most visited place in the Peak District, with an estimated 2 million visitors per year. Malc and I were staying at the Izaac Walton Hotel in the heart of the dale, in a gloriously beautiful spot surrounded by magnificent peaks bathed in golden, very hot, late summer weather. Appropriately named, the Izaac Walton Hotel takes its name from the famous angler, who fished every part of Dovedale and its surroundings.

Izaac was often a guest of the local, lively (polite term) character Charles Cotton, of Beresford Hall in Dovedale. Cotton was a man in continual debt and he used his extensive knowledge of the area, with its nooks, caves and valleys, to hide from his creditors. To Izaac he was a perfect guide and teacher, and he developed his fishing techniques here, becoming an expert fisherman. His famous book *The Compleat Angler* was published in 1653, becoming at the time the most successful book written in the English language. Incredibly, it has never been out of print since.

St Bertram, having lived and died in Ilam, was buried in the local Church of the Holy Cross, once the family chapel of the Russell family. The estate to which it belongs is now a country park owned, along with much of Dovedale, by the National Trust. The church, now part of the Church of England, serves as Ilam Parish Church. The village, still very small, was originally the estate village, with its houses grouped together and built in an unusual, quite ostentatious, ornate style, reminiscent of alpine chalets, looking a little incongruous, but beautiful nonetheless.

Ilam is a typical former estate country park, ideal for walking, and with the River Manifold running through its centre. It is divided neatly into two parts: the woodland on one side of the river and a varied created landscape on the other. There is an Italianate garden, a Lime Tree Walk, a river path and an open space of natural landscape with mature, majestic specimen trees.

The church lies on a flat grassy area close to the River Manifold on the park's south side, quiet and peaceful. Inside, resting in his chapel at the far end of the small church, we find Bertram's shrine.

Although of royal blood, and no doubt known and respected for it, nevertheless Bertram is different from most other Saxon saints. Unlike most, he was not a churchman, monk, abbot or priest – people who are often at the forefront of miracles and healing or simple veneration. Not being part of such a recognised church hierarchy, Bertram must have been truly loved and venerated, his fame spreading quickly and widely after his death. We know this not from records, but because his style of shrine, built in the eleventh century, was a shrine built specifically with pilgrims in mind. So he must have been well established and his village already a popular place of pilgrimage or else this shrine would not have been built in such a way. Bertram's shrine is known as a foramina, and is of an unusual design. Foramina comes from Latin, meaning to be pierced with holes. Bertram's shrine is rare – only three shrines of this type now remain in England, and this is possibly the best. The shrine is raised to around four feet above and surrounding his stone coffin. There are three large holes in each side, and one at the top and bottom. Its age shows in the top, where it is chipped in places and shiny from centuries of pilgrim worship. These holes allowed pilgrims the opportunity to put hands, legs, feet and head through in order to actually touch the stone coffin. Some excitable and desperate pilgrims even attempted to climb completely inside so as to lie on the tomb. If this seems overly strange and ghoulish to us, it was not so in the early Middle Ages. In these early times, and even later too, the vast majority of people had a strong faith and fervently believed in the power of saints to heal, forgive and intercede with Jesus. Even in the midst of life people were concerned about their death, especially believing that their stay in purgatory (a place of waiting after death) could be reduced not only by living a good life, but by intercession, whereby they had a much stronger chance of getting to heaven.

Other ways of doing this were available to the wealthy. They would often pay monks or priests to pray for their own or a loved one's soul after death. Even more extremely, some would establish a chantry in a cathedral or large church set apart, and they paid for prayers to be said in perpetuity. A pilgrimage to a saint often had the same purpose, and for a small donation pilgrims could ask the saint to intercede for them.

How many foramina shrines there were at this time I do not know, but probably many were destroyed. There was certainly one very famous one in Canterbury Cathedral, that of St Thomas à Becket. He was the most popular pilgrimage saint in the early Middle Ages. We know about the pilgrimages to Canterbury from the writings of Geoffrey Chaucer, who immortalised the pilgrim world with his *Canterbury Tales*. His stories, which are actually long poems, take us on a journey from London to Canterbury in the company of pilgrims travelling to Becket's shine. I would take a guess that most people's images of pilgrims are derived from those we meet in Chaucer's tales.

Chaucer lived in the fourteenth century. His birthdate, although unsubstantiated, was between 1341 and 1343. But we do know when he died: 25 October 1400. At around sixty years old he was not an old man, but it would have been considered a good age to reach in those times. Chaucer was very much a Londoner, and there wasn't much he didn't know about the people and places of urban London. He lived in a prime spot, in a house situated on the city walls directly above one of London's main gates – a perfect spot to watch the comings and goings in and out of London. This was a grace-and-favour house. Although we think of Chaucer as a poet, which of course he was, in fact he spent all his adult life as a professional man in many senior capacities and was extremely well connected and affluent. Indeed, for many years he was in the service of kings (at least two), and hence he knew well the routines and gossip of the court.

Although he wasn't a member of the aristocracy he was admired, respected and trusted with important work on behalf of the King, and he was well rewarded for it. We know too that on a number of occasions he was sent on secret missions and embassies, sent personally by the King. There were rumours that he was a king's spy. He may have been, but there is no proof. The fact that he married the sister of Katherine Swinford (later married to John of Gaunt) did his status no harm, and he worked for John of Gaunt too. Chaucer's link to court encouraged him to write, for he was often asked to recite his poetry for the King and his court assembly. His poems were very much in the style of the day, often very long, but Chaucer was different to other contemporary writers because he chose to write in English rather than Latin or Norman French. This proved a major step forward in promoting greater use of English, even at court. Most popular work written centred on court life. Popular at this time were tales of adventure and chivalry, often (as Peter Ackroyd in his biography of Chaucer says) 'tinged by Gothic images with tales of derring-do and travels to distant realms', no doubt partly influenced by the Crusades and knights. From this time we see stories of King Arthur and his knights, with their tales of long and adventurous journeys. These stories sought to stimulate people's imagination, and, though allegorical and apocryphal, they sought to mirror life itself – full of danger, uncertainty and fear, but also containing adventure, discovery and pleasure. Life itself is a pilgrimage.

The *Canterbury Tales*, which he wrote late in life, were of a slightly different ilk, but his knowledge and observation of his native Londoners meant he knew the subject matter would be a hit. He himself knew a great deal about the pilgrim world, particularly the pilgrimage to Becket's shrine. The pilgrim route out of London was a well-trodden one. At this point in his life he had moved from the city and was living in Greenwich, which was then in the country. Greenwich was on the tried-and-tested route, and Chaucer would see pilgrims in various-size groups passing by possibly on a daily basis. No doubt he looked at the people and found ready subject matter for his poems. However, although Chaucer was a religious man, the basis of his new poems was not religion, but rather the journey was a vehicle by which to tell some tales.

So, what are the *Canterbury Tales*? They are a series of separate stories in poetry form, and there are twenty-five in all, about a group of pilgrims (probably reflecting the groups Chaucer was familiar with) who met together at the Tabard Inn in Southwark before setting off on their journey. Like most groups they would have been an excited but motley crew. No doubt some were familiar with each other, but it is likely too that sometimes they were all strangers. Travelling in a group meant they were safer than travelling alone, and there was also the companionship which made the journey interesting. In the *Canterbury Tales* it is suggested at the start that as they travel each person should tell a story, to pass the time and for entertainment. These tales could be serious and noble, truth or fiction, funny or even bawdy. Chaucer knew that his audience would relate to this. We tend to think that people in the past, in different times to our own, were very different from us. But people and their aspirations don't really change. Like us, people in the fourteenth century wanted a home to live in, a job to do, people to talk to, food on the table and to keep in good health and avoid an early death. Despite class divisions, Chaucer's pilgrims were a real assortment, made up of all different types of people and representing all walks of life. There were rich and poor, men and women, knights and peasants, churchmen and administrators, country and city people. Only the very poor would be under-represented, finding it virtually impossible to go on pilgrimage. Cleverly, Chaucer's stories would appeal to all, and those represented have come down to us as a cameo of a group of pilgrims in the early Middle Ages. As such the stories give a clear and hopefully accurate portrayal of pilgrims in medieval society.

After all the tales were told, they would arrive in Canterbury, meeting other pilgrim groups on their way to the cathedral, which at the time was new, large, beautiful and awe-inspiring. Once at the door, what would they find? There would be a lot of people, lots of excited voices, feelings of expectation and wonder, and a reverent but noisy atmosphere. Once inside, there would be a feeling of great anticipation as they made their way to Becket's shrine. The camaraderie of the journey would probably be broken as the group divided itself into friends and social classes. There was probably a queue – people patiently shuffling along, waiting their turn.

Elsewhere there would be hawkers selling souvenirs. Pilgrim badges and vials of Becket's blood (fakes) were popular. There were people selling refreshments and people advertising hostels and guest houses.

Then the pilgrims would reach the shrine. Sadly, we can take the story no further. Today (and for centuries) Becket's shrine no longer exists; however, from writings and stained glass we know that the shrine was a foramina, but with only two large holes on each side. We know how many thousands claimed to be healed. Pilgrims returning to give thanks sometimes brought models of legs and arms to place at the shrine, representing what had been healed. No doubt pilgrims would have been able to touch the shrine. History tells us that the shrine was totally destroyed, deliberately so, at the time of the Reformation (again). Such a saintly relic and the accompanying worship would have been abhorred. This time, however, the destruction probably

St Thomas à Becket window, Canterbury Cathedral, showing foramina shrine.

hadn't been as a result of a direct instruction from King Henry. Rather, it seems that acolytes, incensed after hearing a fiery sermon, were so agitated they broke into the cathedral and smashed the shrine and the earthly remains of Becket himself. Nothing was saved, and sadly today nothing remains. Each day now, a single candle is lit and placed at the spot where his shrine would have been.

So, it is good that we can still see St Bertram's foramina shrine in situ in its original spot, undamaged, having escaped the wrath, fury and vandalism of the Protestant reformers.

A few weeks before setting off for Ilam I had read an article about milestones and the Milestone Society, which preserves these interesting historical artefacts throughout the UK. We can look back to the days before proper roads, before road maps, before people understood geography, before satnavs and before adequate and reliable transport. With our postcodes, satnavs, Ordnance Survey and road maps we take getting from one place to another on a range of different modes of transport for granted. Yet for travellers in former times the introduction of milestones must have seemed a miraculous aid to travel. Stones in various styles with information and direction, sometimes in cast metal, reassured people that they were on the right road. Without signposts or street lights, and with many recognised dangers, they really needed to know where they were and how far they still had to travel. These old milestones are becoming increasingly rare, and as trunk and A-roads are altered, widened and bypassed these interesting signs are continuing to be lost. Since reading about them Malc and I have found ourselves on a journey, eyes peeled, searching the roadsides looking for them. And there aren't that many. Yes, I know we are sad, but it does add an extra interest as we travel. It was a total coincidence that on the road we travelled between Leek in Staffordshire and Ashbourne in Derbyshire, close to Ilam we noticed an exceptionally fine series of metal 'milestones'. All were well maintained, painted and clean and were clearly visible. On close inspection – which meant getting out of the car to look – we could even read who had forged them, and when.

And we are still looking!

Back at the church in Ilam I felt that somehow poor Bertram was not being given the attention he and his shrine deserved. When we first went in I was surprised that there was no indication of where to find him. At the back of the church were displays of cards, postcards and information. Unfortunately, not about Bertram. There were souvenir cards of the headless Saxon crosses in the graveyard and of the ancient font, which with its really old carving seems to display the story of Bertram. Also included was the rather flamboyant and ostentatious marble memorial from the nineteenth century, situated in its own chapel. All of these are, of course, worthy of comment and publicity, but why not anything about Bertram? I was perplexed. It was the same at his shrine. Few people seemed to come in, and again the only information was a really tatty, dirty leaflet suspended on a chain which looked ancient. It was no wonder that those visitors who found their way to the chapel seemed uninterested. Malc and I stayed for a while, even reaching through the holes as the original pilgrims would have done, even taking off my shoes and resting my leg on his tomb. Not surprisingly, I got some rather funny looks. Most people, it seemed, came in, looked quizzically at the shrine, made a cursory walk around the chapel and left. Such a shame! This is a rare piece of church architecture. I found myself talking to people about it and felt a bit like a local guide. Of course I'm not saying that everyone became suddenly fascinated in the way I am, but you could at least see understanding on their faces when I explained. And they also spent longer looking and appreciating.

Back at our hotel in Dovedale, Malc and I decided we really needed to see what the popular walk was like, and to experience that of 2 million other visitors. Close to the start of the walk there was a large car park. There were also two footpaths for those who wanted to make a bit more of both the experience and exercise. One path started in Ilam village, climbing up through fields to a coppice and then down on to the river path. The shorter route went direct from our hotel. It couldn't have been more convenient: out of the hotel door, across the stile into a field to the coppice and the River Dove.

It was a beautiful hot day when we set off, and we soon realised what it meant to be in a beauty spot frequented by so many people. It was very busy, but not uncomfortably so. Where we live in a rather empty Dumfries and Galloway, we are just not used to so many people at one time. As we followed the River Dove in the valley bottom, which is almost gorge-like, being surrounded by the high peaks, we could understand its popularity. It was a flat, easy walk suitable for most people. There were wooded banks, lots of wild flowers and, above all, the river itself. I don't think I have ever seen such a clear, clean, sparkling river as the Dove. The water really did sparkle in the summer sunshine and, fast-flowing, it bubbled along its bed, tumbling over stones – and the bed, free from debris, weeds and moss, was beautifully clear. The main destination for most people is a set of stepping stones across to the other side, with some using them as part of a circular route taking in both sides of the river. Everyone wants to cross the stones, and we were no exception. Being busy, it meant a considerable balancing act when meeting those coming the other way. It was a veritable logjam, but we both made it without wobbling over into the river itself. We noticed on the way back that the National Trust had painted red circles on many trees. These were ash trees suffering from ash dieback and had been marked for felling. Such a shame, especially since new trees planted will not be ash.

Back we went through the copse into the trees and we could see the hotel beckoning us back. It was mid afternoon and the outside beer garden was very inviting. We were stopped by a couple who looked hot and tired, and who were still on their way to the start of the walk.

"Is it far to the start of the walk and the stepping stones?" they asked.

"No, not far, just beyond the copse, and the walk is only about one mile."

"Oh, good. We took the walk up from the village and didn't realise it was so far as well as so hot."

"Well, you are almost there," I reassured them.

We continued whilst the couple remained standing in the field, trying to decide what to do. On reaching our hotel, we looked for them and saw them in the distance, moving on. They had obviously decided to continue.

In the meantime, we relaxed in the hotel garden, enjoying some liquid refreshment, for me, a perfect rejuvenating gin and tonic; a cider for Malc. The sun was still beating down. We looked at the scenery and smiled at each other, knowing we had chosen well; a perfect spot. A hotel waiter came out with a stand of afternoon tea, loaded with sandwiches and cakes and squidgy cream scones, the perfect image of a British summer day, eating afternoon tea in the sunshine in a shady garden. It looked tempting, but it was delivered to the couple on the next table, not us!

We were still drinking as they ate, drank and left. As they

passed our table I asked if they had enjoyed it.

"It looked so delicious," I said.

"Actually, it was rather disappointing," the husband replied. "The sandwiches were really stale."

"Oh, what a pity!" I sympathised. "You should complain."

"Yes, I know, especially as it has cost us £25," he answered dejectedly.

They walked off disgruntled, but I don't think they complained. They should have.

We had been so lucky with the weather in Dovedale, and next day before setting off for home we returned to Ilam Country Park, walking up to and through the Italianate garden. There was a National Trust tea garden high on a terrace overlooking the park, but also offering magnificent views right across the dale. On a slightly lower level was a row of deckchairs. On fine days I imagined people claiming a chair and not moving all day, just relaxing and taking in the views and atmosphere.

We also made our last visit to the church, realising that there are people who know about Bertram and that pilgrims do still come here. Prayer requests had been written and left on top of his shrine. They were interesting, as some examples show:

'I pray for my wife that she will recover from this terrible cancer,' said one.

Another said, 'I pray for peace in the world.'

Then a touching one from a young child: 'I pray for my great-grandad, my guinea pig and three fish and for all creatures who have to die.'

Many of the prayers were addressed directly to St Bertram, so it did seem that the idea of pilgrimage and praying for help from a long-dead saint is still with us.

Our time had run out and we set off for home. Dovedale lies, literally, not just in a valley, but in a deep bowl among the surrounding high peaks. It was a steep drive up from the village in the dale. Stopping at the top, it is virtually impossible to see the valley and Ilam below. They are almost completely hidden, not just by the hills, but because it is so deep as you follow the narrow, twisting roads, trees hiding the view. When we first arrived I couldn't believe how gorgeous it was. The sun was shining in a clear blue sky, and I couldn't believe the awesome view which slowly unfolded the further we went down into the valley.

It seems an odd thing to say when 2 million visitors a year come here, but it nevertheless seems remote, still so hidden. I wondered too how anyone had ever found it in the past. Was this how Bertram's foramina shrine had escaped destruction? So many places, like Canterbury, had been destroyed in the ferment of the Protestant Reformation. People were angry at what they perceived as gross corruption within the Church, with monasteries being singled out by Henry for particular hatred, and it must be said too that the popularity of pilgrimage became included in Henry's wrath. The pilgrim thirst for veneration of saints was perceived to have partly led to this corruption. Pilgrimage and the cult of the relic became a lucrative source of great wealth for those places where saints or relics were buried or kept. Every religious house wanted their relic, which often resulted in their being bought and sold despite very spurious provenance. Certain types of relic were particularly esteemed: Jesus's blood, part of the True Cross, a thorn from the crown of thorns, Mary's tears . . . Logic says to us that these were fakes, but pilgrims and Church leaders did not think this. In general, people wanted to believe that the splinter was a genuine piece of Jesus's Cross. As pilgrims arrived they would give money and gifts, buy souvenirs and pilgrim badges, and the town as a whole would benefit from the pilgrim trade, including buying food and lodging. Everyone stood to gain, and hence people wanted to believe in the power of the relic, the saint and the indulgences sold by clergy to pilgrims, giving them promises which had no basis in truth and which they had no right to offer. Everyone and everywhere wanted their relic and authenticity was greatly subservient to belief.

It cannot be denied that the success and popularity of pilgrimage led to less than honest practices and corruption, yet the original and real purpose of pilgrimage was honourable and continued so, but its popularity certainly declined in post-medieval and Reformation times.

The fact that Bertram's shrine was saved and left in perfect condition is ascribed to what, then? Luck? Insularity? Remoteness? I don't have an answer. The chapel in which he rests was a private chapel on a private estate, so maybe that is another possible reason, as access was not controlled by clergy. Anyway, the fact is that it did survive, and that is good, especially for those of us interested in the pilgrim world. His complete shrine reminds us of all the people hundreds of years ago who came as pilgrims, despite facing a long and possibly arduous journey, time-consuming and perhaps dangerous. Their willingness and urge to come overrode these challenges. They came to seek help, reassurance and healing from a saint revered in his own time as a kind, wise, holy man who knew the experience of tragedy, sadness and regret in his own life. Who are we to judge their motives and ambitions, and how can we know the outcomes of their visits? It was an age of wonder, of miracles and of strong belief, and they believed in and experienced the power of those whom they revered.

The church in Ilam Country Park, where rests St Bertram's tomb.

St Bertram's Well, outside the church at Ilam.

The famous stepping stones across the River Dove, Dovedale, Derbyshire.

Old metal 'milestone' of forged cast iron. One of a sequence along the Leek-to-Ashbourne road.

Heavily carved font of great age, purportedly depicting the life of St Bertram, found in the church at Ilam.

Marilyn, as a pilgrim of old would have done, placing a foot on St Bertram's tomb – seeking healing like thousands of pilgrims in the past.

St Bertram's rare foramina shrine with decorative holes giving pilgrims access to the tomb itself.

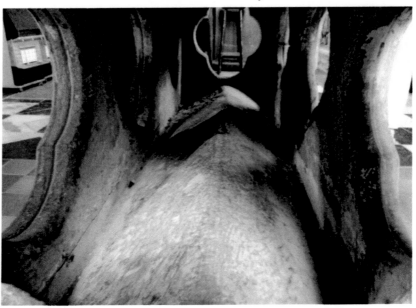

Inside Bertram's foramina shrine, showing the tomb itself.

153

Bertram's foramina shrine with pen and paper to write messages to the saint.

St Bertram's foramina shrine.

154

ST ANDREWS: SHRINE OF SCOTLAND'S PATRON SAINT

Since well before the Norman Conquest St Andrews in Fife has been a famous pilgrimage site. Whether St Andrew's true relics ever rested here is not known, but that people believed them to be his bones is not disputed. It was this certainty that brought thousands of pilgrims over many centuries to worship at his shrine. The development of and importance of the town of St Andrews was a result of these pilgrimages. The church building grew organically, but the final building gave the cathedral the accolade of being the largest in Scotland, having the most prestigious priestly status. Today the cathedral is in ruins, but this does not detract from its sheer size.

But whilst most visitors in the past were pilgrims, the same cannot be said of today. It is a lovely coastal town with seemingly something for everyone: pretty beaches, a harbour, a castle, a cathedral, a university, a lovely centre with character and upmarket shops, and a vibrant, great atmosphere. It is often buzzing with thousands of visitors. Of course one cannot fail to mention golf. Yet it is still a small town which retains its medieval heart and layout as well as period houses and college buildings. There are still only three main streets, two of which lead to and from the cathedral, as they always did. Pilgrims arriving would travel up North Street with the cathedral entrance sited conveniently at the end. After their visit to the shrine they would leave by South Street, either to journey back home or to stay awhile at one of the many hospices and guest houses.

A question I asked myself, though, was do any pilgrims come today to seek out St Andrew the Apostle, or even to visit Scotland's patron saint? Or could it be that Andrew has been lost in his own town?

Andrew was an Apostle of Jesus, possibly the first disciple to be recruited by Him. A fisherman on the Sea of Galilee, he was quickly convinced about Jesus and seemingly left his boat and nets without a qualm when Jesus asked him to follow Him, and to help Him in His ministry. He stayed with Jesus throughout His ministry until the Crucifixion. After this, like the rest of the Apostles, Andrew set out to proclaim Jesus as the Son of God, to convert and bring people to the new and growing Christian faith. It is unclear where Andrew went, but we think that at some point he went to Patras in Greece. We also believe that he too was crucified for his faith. We are told though that he was crucified on an X-shaped cross, as opposed to the more familiar shape. Like Jesus's, it would have been an excruciating death.

Fife, or the Kingdom of Fife, as it is known, lies north and east of Edinburgh across the River Forth. It is a lovely area of Scotland with its own special character, though not in a majestic way. Rather it is a land of undulating hills, rich farmland and many trees, with a mellowness different from the bleakness characterising much of the Scottish Highlands. Along with Perthshire, the next county north of Fife, across the estuary of the River Tay, this is soft-fruit country. There are endless polytunnels producing tons of raspberries and strawberries. The Scottish soft fruit seen in most UK supermarkets will almost certainly be from this eastern area of Scotland. Another notable feature is the East Neuk, comprising a series of small traditional fishing villages, with tiny harbours and small twisting cobbled streets. Unspoilt, they now appeal to the holiday visitor, as opposed to the traditional fisherman. A few boats still ply their trade, catching mainly crabs and lobsters; very different from the heady days of herring fishing and processing along the east coast. These 'silver darlings' were the mainstay of the local fishing economy, and indeed the villages themselves. Sadly, those days are now gone.

St Andrews, at the northern end of Fife, became a centre of pilgrim worship, almost on a par with Rome and Santiago de Compostela in Northern Spain. Only a pilgrimage to Jerusalem would have carried greater kudos to British and European pilgrims. Its importance lay in the fact that here on British soil lay the only relics of an actual Apostle of Jesus. Relics and the shrines they spawned did not come any more important than this. Nowhere else in Britain could claim to house such an important person; a saint, a martyr, someone who actually knew Jesus.

We arrived in St Andrews from the north, from Dundee, across the Tay Bridge. Malc had been wanting a little convertible sports car, not new, just something we could use in nice weather, hood down, enjoying travelling on the lovely and often very empty roads where we live. We bought the car in Dundee and thought it ideal to then travel to St Andrews, a short distance away. Our outward journey had been by train, a pleasant change, travelling from Lockerbie to Edinburgh, then on to Dundee. It was an exciting journey inasmuch as we travelled across the Forth Rail Bridge, now a UNESCO World Heritage Site. It is a unique iron bridge, beautiful in design, and quite astounding. Built in 1890, it is a mile long and a breathtaking example of Victorian architecture.

We would have liked to stay in St Andrews itself, but prices and lack of availability ruled this out. Today more than anything else it seems to be a town of golf! The world's oldest golf club is here, which attracts people from all over the world – modern pilgrims seeking the ultimate game of golf. There are over forty excellent golf courses in the Kingdom of Fife, but none as famous as the 'Old Course' at St Andrews. Its origins go back into the mists of time, and it is possible that it began as long ago as the twelfth century. It was in the eighteenth century, however, when golf as we know it started to take on a universal shape and in 1754 the Royal and Ancient Club in St Andrews became the overall governing body for the sport. Other familiar aspects of the sport, however, took time to become those we are familiar with today. Golf balls, for example, were originally made from wood; later they were stuffed with feathers and were more expensive to buy than the clubs to hit them with! It was only in 1848 that feather balls were replaced by what were called 'gutty' balls, being made from a type of rubber from the Malaysian sapodilla tree. It would be boiled in water for hardening. It became noticeable that if a ball had unintentional dents and marks, then for some reason the ball flew better. People soon started to chip and mark their own balls by hand, and this eventually led to the dimpled ball we are familiar with today. Of course, fast-flying golf balls are still a hazard today, but in golf's early years players traditionally wore red jackets so as to be clearly seen, and hence their jackets acted as a warning to people to be aware of the ball.

When we enquired about hotel prices and availability we were astounded by the prices. At £300-plus per night in many hotels, these were London prices, and we were told that they are virtually fully booked from March to October. This helped confirm the theory that every golfer would, if possible, like to come here, and will pay almost any amount for the privilege.

We lowered our expectations and stayed in a village hotel about a half-hour drive from St Andrews. It was perfectly serviceable and less than a third of the price. These golfers are certainly the new pilgrims, but apart from Malc and me is there any other kind of pilgrims left?

Whilst many doubt that Andrew was really here, is there anything to suggest there is any truth to the claim? And where did the association of St Andrew with the town come from? Most sources tell us his relics were brought here from Southern Europe or Rome. But a remote spot on the Scottish east coast is not only a long way from the dry Mediterranean countries, but rather unlikely too. There is no real evidence or proof that St Andrew's remains were ever here, but this is the same with most 'relic' shrines. But people believed that they were his, and this powerful belief was sufficient to bring thousands of pilgrims here over many centuries. The fact that both his bones and his shrine were totally destroyed, dispersed and lost does not help. What we do know is that the relics lay in a special shrine below the cathedral's high altar. This area, like much else, is in ruins and nothing remains. Nevertheless, the cathedral and the town itself grew up around the Apostle. When completed, the cathedral was the largest in Scotland and was reputedly magnificent, and the link with Andrew made it the most important pilgrimage site, not just in Scotland, but in Britain and even Europe.

Despite the uncertainty of 'Whose bones?', there was said, in the early days of the Saxon period, that there was some real provenance about the relics. Two main theories came to prominence. The first centres around a mysterious figure, St Rule. He had no links with Britain and was said to be from Southern Europe, where he claimed to have acquired Andrew's skeletonised bones from Patras in Greece. Setting sail, he had no idea where he ought to go and wandered far north until shipwrecked on the North Fife coast.

In the grounds of the cathedral is the oldest building, known as St Rule's Tower, so there must have been enough people who believed him for a church to hold the relics to have been built in his name. Nevertheless, this version of how Andrew came here is thought by many to be fanciful.

A second, later theory, but still early in the eighth century, is about St Wilfrid. We first met Wilfrid in Hexham, at the abbey where he was a bishop. His specially built chapel, to which pilgrims flocked, held relics which he and the pilgrims believed to be those of St Andrew. His chapel was known as St Andrew's Chapel. At some point after Wilfrid's death these relics disappeared. But were they those of St Andrew? The only fact which gives even a modicum of possibility is that we know Wilfrid was a great traveller. Unlike many in the north of England who were of the Celtic tradition, Wilfrid was staunchly pro-Roman. He journeyed several times to Rome and had audiences with the Pope. These visits may have been sycophantic, using his support of Popes and the Roman Church to further his career – a successful move on Wilfrid's part as it led to him achieving wealth and lucrative bishoprics. If he brought back to Hexham some of Andrew's bones, then it would seem that the bones had been in Rome, of which there is no proof whatsoever, although it was thought that they may have come to Rome from Patras or even via Constantinople. If this was so, then poor Andrew certainly travelled a great deal after his death, and what appears worse is that his skeleton would have been broken up and various parts dispersed to many places, carried by various priests.

The next episode concerns a Bishop Acca, who succeeded Wilfrid at Hexham, where Acca's beautiful high stone cross still stands in Hexham Abbey. Acca became an exile and he apparently journeyed to St Andrews. But he was not leaving Hexham without the relics. He took with him what he believed to be Andrew's bones. These then came to rest and remained until destruction in the Scottish Reformation. Henceforth, they came to be regarded as the relics of St Andrew and became the focus of pilgrimage. They were the making of Andrew as Scotland's patron saint.

There were many other pilgrim sites in Fife, and the Fife Pilgrim Way became extremely popular. It would have been the route taken by most whose intended destination was St Andrews. Most would travel north from today's Edinburgh to the River Forth. The crossing of the river estuary became easier when Queen Margaret of Scotland established a ferry for the benefit of pilgrims. This ferry went from South to North Queensferry, towns named after this beloved queen. She was herself a pious woman and she later became a saint, her shrine at Dunfermline becoming a pilgrim site, and added to the Pilgrim Way. She established the ferry sometime after 1070, after her marriage to King Malcolm. The fact that a ferry was deemed useful for pilgrim travellers shows that these pilgrim journeys were already well established and pilgrims numerous. Certainly it would seem that the relics had been there for a long time, their reputation undisputed.

This making of pilgrim journeys easier is a feature of many such trips, reflecting on the fact that in these early times pilgrims had a hard, arduous, often long and sometimes expensive journey. Yes, it was a purposeful adventure, but it was as hazardous as it was exciting. So it was important to be properly prepared. Hospices and guest houses provided hospitality, but there were many other things to consider, first and foremost, the recommendation to travel in groups for increased safety. So popular was pilgrimage that a guide was drawn up to help them prepare properly. This guide gave advice on the safest way to travel, where to stay and what to expect when you reached your destination. There was even a standard mode of dress and advice on what to take. Pilgrims were advised to take a hat, a staff, appropriate clothing and shoes, and a scrip (a bag for essentials), and to ensure money was kept in a safe place. Travel guides, it seems, are not a modern invention at all. But as well as this excellent advice, pilgrims couldn't set off without knowing how to get to their destination and how long it might take. Many people setting off might never have previously left their town or village, were possibly illiterate, not rich and had little or no sense of geography. There were no accurate maps, roads were poor or non-existent and most people would walk.

One person who understood how difficult it could be to find the way was a St Albans monk, Matthew Paris. It was the mid thirteenth century and pilgrimage to the Holy Land was the one most pilgrims aspired to undertake, yet in reality few did. It was at the time of the Crusades with ongoing battles between Christians and Muslims. Not only was it an arduous journey of several months, but the Holy Land was a highly unstable and dangerous region. Matthew Paris could not control every facet of the pilgrim journey, but what he did do was to draw up maps and itineraries for pilgrims to follow, starting from London right to Jerusalem. It may still have presented many dangers, but at least they had a clearer idea of which way to go. Matthew himself never went to Jerusalem, and is thought to have determined the best route by asking those who had been for details of the journey. Matthew would have been familiar with pilgrimage, however, though within a smaller geographic area.

St Albans, where he was based as a monk, housed a hugely popular shrine, that of St Alban, Britain's first Christian martyr. His shrine also has a link with St Andrews in that their shrines were of a very similar type. The relics were placed in an ornate reliquary (a special casket for bones), placed on the stone shrine and covered with a colourful, highly embellished canopy in the shape of a ridged roof. In St Albans Cathedral there is an uncommon feature of a 'watching' gallery. So precious was the shrine, and so fearful were they of desecration, that all the time pilgrims were coming and going they would be closely watched.

Also, the reliquary would be well hidden under its canopy,

providing no real access to the saint's relics. At St Andrews an intricate system of pulleys was attached to the canopy, enabling it to be lifted up and down, revealing the sacred reliquary with the saint's bones inside. On certain special occasions, important visitors were invited to attend this uncovering, with bells being rung and the atmosphere charged with anticipation. As the canopy lifted, the visitors would be allowed to see the reliquary and, on even more-special occasions, to even see the bones inside. The whole place surrounding the shrine would be crowded, people jostling each other in order to see what was happening. Emotions would run high with tears, pilgrims bowing and kneeling to venerate this most holy of saints. However, the Church ensured that the ordinary pilgrim was kept at a considerable distance from this special event.

It was a beautiful sunny day in St Andrews as we strolled in the huge cathedral ruins fanning out from the town to the harbour and beach in a glorious setting. We headed to the visitor centre and museum, a fascinating display awaiting. Despite the very busy town, the museum was quiet.

Comprising many stone crosses and grave slabs, I watched people as they came in and paid their money. So many walked quickly around, had a cursory look and looked askance at most things. Their expressions said, "Oh, this is boring, nothing but bits of old stone. What a waste of money!" and they went back out to see the cathedral ruins instead. I found it all very interesting, especially the display of old gravestones, mostly from the sixteenth century, which have been found at various times in the cathedral grounds. In the Middle Ages, people's faith was strong; heaven and hell were very real to them. Introduced probably by the Knights Templar in Jerusalem, the phrase 'memento mori' was common. Meaning literally 'remember you will die', this was a constant reminder that if people wanted to go to heaven, then they would need to make amends before they died. Pilgrimage was an important way to do this, by seeking forgiveness from a favourite saint, making promises to reform, paying for indulgences, promising forgiveness or taking on long and difficult journeys. These were all ways in which a person could be redeemed so as to avoid going either to purgatory or, indeed, even straight to hell. The gravestones in the museum show images of 'memento mori', still prevalent in the sixteenth century. These gravestones clearly belonged to former wealthy people, so they are large and elaborately carved. The various motifs are common to all – skulls and crossbones, hourglasses, spades and shovels (representing gravediggers). The carvings are elaborate and extremely well executed. Together they gave a message to all who passed by: Remember you will die. This is where, like me, you will end up! Macabre, yes, but it is also great art.

I hadn't associated this area with the Picts, but Fife was indeed part of 'Pictland'. The Picts remain a mysterious people, and we don't know what these older inhabitants of Scotland actually called themselves. Pict is a Roman name meaning 'painted people', for their habit of painting their faces. They had no form of writing, so their history and culture has to be gleaned in other ways. But they had great artistic talent and the remaining Pictish stones scattered around Eastern Scotland are a testament to their great skill in carving. When they were converted to Christianity, reputedly by Columba, they transferred these skills to Christian carvings. A huge sarcophagus in another part of the museum was discovered here, and is recognised as one of the most magnificently carved slabs of early medieval times in the whole of Europe. Who the sarcophagus was made for is not known, but the quality indicates it must have been for someone of very high status, maybe a Pictish king or even St Andrew himself!

And speaking of Andrew, where was he in this museum? Sadly, I couldn't find anything which related to him. There is mention of him in the official guidebook, but on-site he was invisible. I even had to ask where the shrine would have been. "Close to the high altar," I was told. Right. Still not clear, and there was no plaque to indicate the spot at all. I had the distinct feeling that Andrew had in fact been lost, not just literally, in respect of the relics, but metaphorically too.

Outside of St Andrews, is this the case? Across Scotland, has St Andrew been forgotten?

In 1995, a poll by the *Scotland on Sunday* newspaper found that only thirty-nine per cent knew the date of St Andrew's Day (30 November).

In 1994, the then First Minister, Alex Salmond, said this: "While other countries celebrate their national day in style, St Andrew is relegated to B-league status in his adopted homeland. Compared to Burns Night and Hogmanay, the feast day of St Andrew hardly gets a look-in."

A Mr Graham Birse said, "Tartan is more likely to be recognised overseas than the Saltire*."

The Reverend Professor Robin Barber goes even further, saying, "It seems to me that now the actual figure of St Andrew really has no significance for Scotland . . . the thistle probably means more to most Scots than their patron saint."

I suppose in truth this is no different to the English recognition of St George and his day (23 April). How many people recognise that today?

It is still sad though about St Andrew, when Scotland is one of very few countries in the world that has an Apostle of Jesus as its patron saint.

We walked on to look at the rest of the town, a hive of activity. On North Street we spotted a café calling us in for a cup of tea called the North Port Café. We realised that in fact this was the café regularly frequented by William and Kate early in their relationship when students at St Andrews University; another reason why St Andrews' profile has recently been raised.

On to the castle in a prominent position on a crag overhanging the sea, but this was not a fortress castle; rather it was the residence of the Archbishops of St Andrews for hundreds of years. It was a sinecure of great luxury, being the most prestigious Church position in Scotland, and lucrative too.

In the grounds we could hear voices and the smell of barbecued food was rising up from the beach below. We looked over the castle wall to see families sunning themselves, searching rock pools, swimming in the sea and even cooking their lunch, and very good it smelled too.

The 'bottle' dungeon belonging to the castle was far less

* The blue and white flag of Scotland.

an attraction than the beach. This deep, dark, damp hole in the ground, shaped as its name suggests, is a gruesome reminder of the penalty people paid for their misdemeanours, a shocking memorial to the conditions people were subjected to, even those whose only crime was the poaching of a rabbit, for example. They knew, once thrown in, they would never see daylight again, and so opposite from the luxury and affluence enjoyed by the churchmen only a few yards away.

Before heading back to the car we went to see the eighteenth hole of St Andrews Ancient and Royal Golf Club. The strangest thing which struck Malc and me is that it is literally right in the middle of town, with people strolling or rushing by, cars passing on both sides whilst players nonchalantly ignore all the activity going on around them and continue playing this very important hole. Then, looking round proudly, they can say to themselves, "Yes, I really have just played a round of golf on this the most prestigious course in the world." And they will sigh with contentment.

So people arrive; to play golf, to attend the university, to sit on the beach, to shop in the upmarket town, to stroll around the lovely massive ruins, and to do the tour of the numerous sites.

To see where St Andrew the Apostle's shrine was? Mmm – I'll hold the page on that one.

The ruins of St Andrew's Cathedral, with St Rule's Tower, a precursor of the cathedral.

Old representation of definitive example of a Celtic Christian cross in St Andrews Cathedral Museum.

Undercroft at St Andrews Cathedral with a collection of 'memento mori' gravestones with striking carvings.

Celebrated Pictish sarcophagus in the museum at St Andrews Cathedral, Fife.

Pans o pilgrim
that passeth by this way
upon mine end
and thou sal lear to sin
and think also, upon the latter day
when thou (to god) man count
then best (thou now) begin.

A PERSONAL PILGRIMAGE: ABERDOUR, FIFE

After St Andrews we set off for home, but then made an unscheduled stop in Aberdour, on the southern coast of Fife. It is an unspoilt town with castle and harbour and its famous Silver Sands beach. But, for me, Aberdour is more than just another Fife tourist town.

As a young girl I was poorly for many years with severe asthma, limiting my life as well as my education. I didn't give in to it and tried to follow my friends in their many hobbies and activities. After the Brownies I joined the Girl Guides along with my friend Janice. This was in deepest polluted Wigan, and every year our Guides company went on a camping holiday for two weeks in the summer break. It was always to Aberdour, camping in a farmer's field just out of town and on a rise. How they ever found out about this place I don't know. It was a lovely town and still is.

I struggled to breathe every day, but my worried parents didn't want to stop me doing things and going places, so to Aberdour I went. In their concern, however, my parents booked a holiday in the same area at Burntisland, just down the coast, so they could keep an eye on me. I don't understand why, but the Guiders were real bullies and were really intolerant of my illness and very uncaring, and I was often humiliated. Every Sunday we would all go to church in town, walking in formation. Because I couldn't breathe, and had to walk very slowly, they made me set off much earlier, on my own, so I wouldn't hold them up! Why couldn't they suggest we all left earlier so we could be together? I believe it was to make me feel set apart. They eventually met me in church. I remember feeling acutely embarrassed by being singled out like this, as any teenager would. I hated the Guides and don't know why I put up with it, but I loved Aberdour. This was a perfect opportunity to see it again; not to remember the sad times, but to see it with different eyes many years later. Quite unexpectedly, I found out that the Church of St Fillan had been a centre of pilgrimage, which fitted right in.

Malc and I set off to find the church, and what a lovely spot! Located at the side of the castle, with views over the Forth Estuary, and distant views over to the Pentland Hills beyond Edinburgh, it was indeed lovely. High walls kept it sheltered, and on the day we visited it was warm and very pleasant.

St Fillan's is an old Norman church and is very beautiful. Much of the inside retains its Norman details, and the chancel appears almost untouched. It is considered to be one of Scotland's most beautiful churches, and I couldn't disagree. The setting, the building itself and its history all added to its beautiful ambiance. Yet what you see is misleading, for in the 1920s this church was a roofless ruin, after which, with great devotion and faith, it was rebuilt as it looked before. Dating from the early twelfth century, there may well have been an earlier church on the site, and for many centuries it was linked with the abbey on Inchcolm Island, a short distance away by ferry in the Firth of Forth. There is a story which tells of King Alexander I, who on travelling from the Queen's ferry was driven to the island in a storm. Believing that this saved his life, he promised to establish an Augustinian monastery on the island and it benefited from royal endowments in the future. Canons from the monastery were directly involved in the running of the church. It was dedicated to St Fillan very early; but as there appears to have been more than one St Fillan associated with the area, it is unclear where each St Fillan fits with each dedicated church.

An interesting anecdote relates to a church endowment from James Douglas, Laird of Dalkeith, knight, in 1390. Douglas named the church in his will, and it is believed to be the oldest extant will made by a Scotsman. The church guide relates this in full, including in Latin, but in the English translation it says, 'Sir James left £3 6s. 8d. to the church for the purchase of a vestment.'

A short distance from the church was a well which was found to have healing qualities, particularly for eye complaints. It became well known, and the number of pilgrims increased. There must have been a considerable number because around 1474 land was granted to found a hospice known as the Hospital of St Martha. Here pilgrims could take respite from their journey as they sought healing from the well, which is now no longer in existence. Part of Aberdour's popularity for pilgrims was that it was very much part of a well-established pilgrim route. Beginning with St Margaret's shrine in Dunfermline, the journey having been made easier since the start of the ferry across the Forth Estuary, they would continue on through Fife to their journey's end, probably St Andrews. Further down the Fife coast at the old fishing village of Pittenweem was another stopping-off place. Here was St Fillan's cave, though it may well have been a different St Fillan from that at Aberdour. This cave is associated with hermits who greeted pilgrims on their way. The cave, which is still accessible, is thousands of years old, and at this continued place of pilgrimage people are welcome to share in the experience of a special place with its centuries of history and worship.

Back at Aberdour Church is another lovely artefact, the Pilgrim Stone. How old it is isn't known, and it was probably originally in a different place. Today it sits on the outside wall of the church, much of its writing having been eroded and obscured over time. The wording on the stone slab is very much in the style of a memento mori (remember, you will die), with people wanting to clear their slate of sins and transgressions within their lifetime.

The inscription reads:

'Pans o pilgrim [pans meaning think]
that passeth by this way
upon thine end
and thou sal fear to sin
and think also, upon the latter day
when thou (to God) man count
then best (thou now) begin.'

It was a warning of which many pilgrims would take serious note.

Royalty throughout the ages believed in pilgrimage. They may have had a favourite saint or a place known for a special purpose. Often they would pray for success in battle, for the safety of the army, as well as contemplate over difficult

Definitive style for Celtic crosses in a beautiful modern window in St Fillan's church, Aberdour, Fife.

decisions. Robert the Bruce, remembered from the Scottish Wars of Independence and the famous Battle of Bannockburn, was one such king who believed in the power of saints. Going into battle at Bannockburn he was said to have carried a relic, the arm of St Fillan, with him. After the battle Robert the Bruce reputedly came to St Fillan's to pray and give thanks for the success.

However, even a king can be denied access to a church, and this is the case with Bruce. He suffered from leprosy, and whatever his status he was not allowed to mingle with others, the fear of leprosy was so great. In Aberdour Church is a 'leper squint' or window. Whilst not unknown today, they are nevertheless uncommon. There would be a small opening or window made into the church fabric, outside which the leper would stand, converse, seek healing or listen to the Mass.

We tend to think of leprosy as a condition of ancient and more primitive times and now no longer relevant in our modern world. In the New Testament Jesus is often shown as healing lepers. They were desperate people, shunned, shut away, stigmatised, unable to work. People were extremely afraid of leprosy. Leprosy has not gone away. The Leprosy Mission charity works across the world today where leprosy is present, and this is in 143 countries. There are over 2 million sufferers worldwide and new cases are being diagnosed daily. Ignorance of the disease means today's sufferers still experience the same stigmas as they did 2,000 years ago. Leprosy devastates people's lives. Even in the UK there were five reported cases in 2017. In the Middle Ages the number was much higher. Leprosy was common and there was no cure and anyone could become a leper. Indeed, the word 'leper' itself has connotations and the word comes down to us as someone shunned. No one wants to know them and they are outside society. For many sufferers pilgrimage was the last resort in their attempt at healing. But they could not travel with other pilgrims and we read in history of lepers approaching a village and ringing a bell to warn people of their approach. On hearing the bell villagers would scatter until the lepers had passed through. Monasteries would often offer to care for lepers and offer accommodation on their journey. But there were many lepers, and often hospices and hospitals were built specially along pilgrim routes. When even a king with leprosy was not allowed to mingle with others then ordinary people had no chance. It is no wonder they had so much faith in saints, wells and relics, for it was virtually their last chance not only of healing, but of once more being allowed to return to the company of others. How many were ever healed is not known, but the squint still seen in Aberdour Church is an acute reminder of those people and the dreadful fear it engendered in the lives of so many ordinary people.

Aberdour had been all the good things I remembered from years ago, and seeing it through older eyes helped me cancel out the bitter memories. This was me now, a different person yet visiting a small town very much unchanged and glad I made the effort to go. I may never see it again!

ST EDMUND'S HAND: LANCASHIRE

Part One

A Catholic church in the heart of heavily urbanised Lancashire is not the first place anyone would think to look for a curious relic, venerated for its healing powers. Hemmed in by the busy M6 motorway and the A58, the Church of St Oswald and St Edmund Arrowsmith stands tucked into its own leafy oasis. Just a couple of hundred yards away is the centre of what was once the independent bustling market town of Ashton-in-Makerfield. Having been swallowed up by the large adjacent town of Wigan, it soon became part of the vast Lancashire coalfield in the nineteenth century and was subject, like most places, to considerable expansion. Nevertheless, Ashton has, against all the odds, managed to retain its own identity. With its small one-street town centre, it is not exactly thriving, but it is at least surviving. Its weekly market too is just hanging on. Yet within walking distance of this unassuming town, in the tranquillity of the nearby church, the preserved hand of St Edmund Arrowsmith resides in peace and solitude, as it has for many years.

Catholicism has always been strong in the Wigan area, so it is not so surprising to find that many old houses retain secret priest holes. At times when it was illegal to admit belonging to the Catholic faith and dangerous to be caught practising it and attending Mass, believers had to find unusual and idiosyncratic ways of maintaining their faith. Wealthy families would be able to secrete priests in their houses, but ordinary people could not do this. Other imaginative and courageous ways were found, however. One such secret scheme can be found in the village of Standish, close to Wigan. Here there is a house called Cat-in-the-Window Farm, and according to local legend this building was used by its owner to conduct illegal Mass. When a priest became available, the owner would place a picture of a cat in the window. When local residents saw this, they knew it was a signal that they could attend Mass. Afterwards, the cat would be removed until the next time. The house today has three cats painted on the outside wall to commemorate this strange story and the bravery of remarkable ordinary people who risked their lives for their faith.

So to find the relic of a recusant priest who was executed for his faith is not really such a surprise in this part of Lancashire. What happened to this priest after his death is, however, a remarkable story.

Malc and I arrived at this church on a Saturday lunchtime, when, as on every other Saturday, St Edmund is venerated. I was, of course, unsure what to expect. But I realised that although the occasion seemed somewhat understated, I was actually witnessing an event that has happened in exactly the same way for hundreds of years.

The church itself is huge and beautiful in an austere Norman style, with decorative chevron pillars and primitive-looking sculptures. The ceiling is memorable, decorated, with three alcoves painted to resemble a night sky. Outside, its square tower looks like an Italian campanile.

Malc and I are not familiar with the Catholic Mass and found it hard to follow, even with a word sheet to help us. There were about thirty people in the church – clearly regulars, not needing any sheet, knowing the entire liturgy by heart. We were a little embarrassed, but managed to stand up and sit down in the right places, so it was OK in the end. But so far there had been no sign of Edmund's 'holy hand'. We waited, and then at the end of the Mass we noticed people starting to leave their seats and walk towards the altar. We followed. This was the veneration. The priest held up a glass globe. We were too far away to see it clearly, but inside the globe was the hand. As each person in turn approached, the priest pressed the globe against their forehead, wiped the glass and moved on to the next person. Of course the same thing happened to Malc and me. It all happened so quickly, it was over before I could appreciate what had just happened. This had been an action venerating a man who had died for his faith and also an opportunity to acknowledge his healing power. What didn't occur to me until afterwards was that I had just been blessed by a 400-year-old hand! A very strange experience, certainly, but actually not an unpleasant one.

This hand was indeed old, for Edmund Arrowsmith was executed in 1628 at Lancaster on John of Gaunt Hill, named after the once powerful Duke of Lancaster. Edmund was dragged to the place of execution on a willow hurdle, then hanged, drawn and quartered. This happened during the reign of King Charles I, at which time it was still illegal to train as a Catholic priest in Britain and, equally, also illegal to partake in the Catholic Mass. Anyone wishing to become a priest had only one option: to travel secretly to France, where they could be ordained. Edmund followed this practice, returning to Lancashire to serve a local community in the rural area around Chorley*. Of course it was a secret life, for priests lived in constant fear of being discovered celebrating the Mass. If found doing so, the priest would face the death penalty. Edmund's last Mass was conducted in the secret attic of a house in rural Brindle, a small village north of Chorley. His fear of exposure was justified when, as a result of a disagreement with two aggrieved parishioners, he was betrayed to the authorities, later being sentenced to death. This was a travesty to most people who knew Edmund. He had been greatly loved and respected, and it was virtually impossible to find a man who would hang him. At no point, either during his mockery of a trial, or as he awaited his death, did he admit to having done wrong. After his execution, and the devastating treatment of his body afterwards, it is astonishing that his hand was retrieved.

I spoke to the church priest, Father Newins, at the end of the service and discussed what had happened to Edmund. He said

* Chorley is a market town between Wigan and Preston.

that on his mother's side, Edmund was a member of a prominent local family, the Gerards of Bryn. They were a powerful aristocratic family and had lived and owned land in the area for hundreds of years. They were wealthy too. Fast-forward into the nineteenth century: the Gerards were still prominent and were to become one of the wealthiest families in the north of England when rich seams of coal were found on their land at Bryn and the surrounding area. Bryn is a small town between Wigan and Ashton. This ancient family was reputed to be of royal blood, being directly descended from the Plantagenet King Henry II. The Gerards had been fervent Catholics for hundreds of years and Edmund was not the first to be involved in Catholic plots and scandals. For Edmund to have been betrayed and killed thus would have incensed this powerful family. They undoubtedly had influence in many places and they were apparently able to discover where Edmund's remains had been taken. Anecdotally, it seems that contacts in the hierarchy secreted them to where he lay, and they were at least able to return with his hand. The family took his hand back to the Gerard family home at Bryn Hall, where they wrapped it in silk and placed it in a wooden box and there it remained with the family. When some decades later a family member inspected the hand, it was found to be uncorrupted, not mummified, for there was still flesh. From this point, the family promoted what they considered to be a miracle and it became the 'holy hand'. His story moved on when claims of healing occurring in the presence of the hand or as a result of praying to him grew over time. Eventually the Gerards gave money to build a church where Edmund's hand could be kept.

Father Newins told me, however, that "It was a very long time before he was canonised. It was only in 1970 he became a saint and this was because of proven miracles, not because of his martyrdom."

I asked him if I could take a closer look at the hand. Father Newins brought it to me, but I was not allowed to touch it – understandable really. I found out later from one of his parishioners that Father Newins had not long since been held at gunpoint and robbed. After this shocking and terrifying experience, even though there was no evidence that they wanted to damage or steal the hand, nevertheless it was thought sensible to improve security. Edmund was given his own safe and now only emerges on his veneration days, and then is quickly locked up again.

At this point I noticed that Malc had done a bit of a disappearing act, ostensibly to wander around the church. I knew, though, that he didn't want to be too close to the hand; but for me, seeing it, I thought it was simply amazing. This was the first time I had ever looked closely at a relic, or indeed anything remotely like this. In the past I have seen mummies in the Egyptian galleries in museums, but they somehow seemed removed and unreal. I reminded myself that this is the actual hand of a dead priest from more than 400 years ago. It seemed very real, its impact greater because I knew who it was. Was it scary? I would have to say no! It was remarkably well preserved, if just a little shrunken, and how it has remained so well preserved is not known. It is clearly his right hand with the thumb and fingers slightly bent. The nails were intact, with his fingerprints still clearly visible. Yes, it was something of a strange experience, but far from spooky or abhorrent; rather, I think I felt somewhat awed, both by the hand itself and by the emotions it has and still does engender in the hearts and minds of believers.

The people of the congregation were very friendly. I expected this since Wiganers, like most northerners, are known for their friendliness and warmth. I asked one woman as we came out of church how much had Ashton changed over the years?

She told me, "It's been hard to keep its identity, made harder by the ever increasing developments, which blur boundaries, places merging into one another. And, like everywhere else, we are losing traditional and independent shops, losing out to the same names found in every other town. But at the moment," she emphasised, "the biggest bone of contention here is the proposed conversion of the old Victorian town hall into a medical centre. Everyone is opposed to it. There is nowhere to park, access is really poor and it is a rabbit warren of small, dark rooms."

Ah, the town hall! Now, I know about this because some

years ago when I worked for Wigan Council I was based at Ashton Town Hall. Despite its age, it has nothing memorable or noteworthy about it, having no architectural merit. It is also seemingly tagged on to the end of an insignificant street attached to an equally unremarkable building. It was notoriously poky, and my office was tucked away in the rabbit warren. I remember one day I was expecting a colleague for a meeting. He hadn't been before, and he was late and flustered when he arrived.

"Good grief, Marilyn!" he exclaimed. "Osama bin Laden could hide out here and nobody would find him!"

And we both laughed.

Malc and I had a quick walk around the little town, noting elements of Edmund's ancestors in Gerard Street and the Gerard Arms, and then finding a cup of tea in a little café. Then, before heading home, we went back to the church, wanting to see the grottos we had noticed earlier, sitting in a peaceful garden area within the graveyard. We noticed a woman who had been in church, standing by a grave, trowel in hand. We discussed the overgrown grave she was attending.

"This is the grave of a former priest," she said. "I like to keep it tidy."

These parishioners seemed very devoted Catholics living in a small, insignificant town to which they were very attached. As Malc and I drove away I felt a warmth for the little town. It isn't a place people would normally seek out. It isn't beautiful and parts are still blighted by its industrial past, but it is lived in by warm, welcoming people with an enduring loyalty to their town, church, priesthood and special saint. I really felt that they deserve their saint, and long may he continue to reside and be venerated there.

There is a postscript to this visit. In truth, I never really expected anything to happen and was totally unprepared for what I experienced when I got home. After a week I felt noticeably different. It wasn't healing in the strict sense, but I felt uplifted, peaceful, content, more at one with myself and my world, leading to a feeling of a great well-being. I didn't want to mention it to Malc, feeling perhaps a little bit foolish. Then, as the feeling continued, I found myself telling him late one night whilst reading in bed. And – the strangest thing! – Malc said he had felt exactly the same, but hadn't wanted to say anything. So was it a placebo effect, spiritual strengthening or a miracle? We choose to believe the latter. You may not, of course!

Part Two

When Malc and I visited Ashton for the weekly veneration of Edmund's hand, we didn't expect to go back again. However, Father Newins had earlier mentioned to us that an annual pilgrimage is held on St Edmund's feast day, 28 August. Thinking this might be interesting, and wondering how different it might be to the weekly event, we decided to go back. After all, it wasn't that far. I was curious about how many people would be there and where they had come from. Would it be an international event? There are still many pilgrimages today, but I had been thinking that quite possibly the veneration of the holy hand is unique in Britain. As far as I am aware, no true relic still exists today, let alone its continued veneration over hundreds of years. Yes, there are still tombs and shrines, as at Durham with Cuthbert and Bede and Kentigern in Glasgow, but not relics as seen and touched in Ashton. If it is unique in these times, I question the fact of its being tucked away in relative obscurity and why more people don't know about it. His pilgrimage day would hopefully give me an idea of how far and wide he is recognised. Edmund's hand is a unique and fascinating link to the late Middle Ages and its obsession with pilgrimage. Yet Edmund is also still very much a part of today; even part of the daily lives of Ashton's residents. They still believe in the mystery and power of spiritual healing.

Despite our NHS, medical science and complementary therapies, there may still be other ways of healing. And who is to say that it doesn't work? People talk of the efficacy of homeopathic medicine, but if it does work no one really understands why. Is this so very different to spiritual healing, which comes with the Christian faith? This can seem so powerful, with God instigating healing through what was once one of his faithful servants, in this case, St Edmund. Well, I don't know, but I have been willing to give it a try. So once again Malc and I were on the familiar M6 on a busy bank-holiday weekend. It was especially busy when we reached the turn-off for the M55 at Preston, the road taking visitors to Blackpool.

From the end of August to the end of November, most visitors would be going to see the lights, or Blackpool Illuminations, as they are properly known. This trip by millions of people is a true Lancashire pilgrimage, as popular today as when they were first lit up in 1912. Most Lancastrians would say there is nothing like the atmosphere on Blackpool Promenade at night with the lights twinkling as everyone eats their fish and chips. One million lights are lit each year, taking twenty-two weeks to put up and fourteen to take down. Additional attractions include the old Blackpool trams, which are covered with lights in the shapes of a rocket, ship and train. People still queue to ride on them, even though once on you can't see the shape, but a tram tour of the lights is something you really need to do. Blackpool Tower is also lit up, and at 600 feet high it can be seen up to thirty miles away. Since 1934, a celebrity has always switched on the lights. One of the more famous and eccentric was Red Rum after he won the Grand National. However, he apparently had a difficulty with the switches! It costs £2.4 million to stage each year, and this number is only beaten by the average 3.4 million visitors who give a massive boost to the town's economy.

Ours, of course, was something of a different pilgrimage, albeit in the same county, and it wasn't long before we were once again driving up to the church, well in time for the service at 4 p.m. Once again we commented on the church's beautiful interior, and I had found out that in fact it is considered one of the most beautiful Catholic churches in England. If my humble opinion is worth anything, it deserves the accolade. Sitting by us in the same pew was Pauline, whom we had met on our previous visit. She told us about the church and that, despite the Romanesque architectural style, it was only built in the twentieth century on the site of a previous church. At the time it was built, it was very much a community effort, with many local people helping with the building work.

"My great-grandfather was one of the volunteers who helped," Pauline told us proudly.

She was also thrilled to tell us that this same week her daughter had been married in St Edmund's and was the fifth generation of her family to do so.

The church rapidly filled up, and as the service started Malc did a rough count. Around 300 people were present. The whole event was a more formal and flamboyant affair, being quite a spectacle, with four priests involved in the service, hymns, a choir and even the singing of a specially written hymn for St Edmund's Day. The singing was robust and the atmosphere charged, although the veneration proved to be exactly the same as before. As a result, Malc and I were pleased with ourselves because this time we knew what to do.

The event concluded with everyone being invited to the parish rooms for tea and biscuits. Of course this perennially English tradition must be upheld. Over tea we spoke again to Pauline, who wanted to tell us more about her daughter's wedding. She had given her away and also gave a speech.

"Would you like to hear it?" she asked us.

How could we say no! "That would be lovely," we said.

She immediately whipped a copy of the speech from her bag. She had been carrying it around in case anyone wanted to hear it, or perhaps people like us who were willing to listen! She was so clearly still on a real high from the wedding – she was glowing with pride. It was lovely to see someone so happy.

When we managed to find a seat, we sat with Naina and her husband, who had also sat in our pew, and we started chatting. They lived in Ashton and had done so all their lives, but they were not Catholics and had never been to the healing service before.

"My husband is not well," Naina told us, "and quite out of the blue he said, 'Shall we go to the healing?'"

Which they did.

She told us too that St Edmund is very well known locally and there are many stories, many of which seem to prove his healing powers.

Before leaving, I wanted to speak to Father Newins. He was pleased, he said, with the number of people in church this year, which seemed markedly up on previous years. When I explained that Malc had counted around 300, he was really pleased.

"In general, though, the numbers are on the decrease," he said.

I asked him, "Where do the pilgrims come from?" hoping for a wide spread of locations.

"Oh, they are mostly local, and then some come from Wigan – even some from as far as Liverpool."

Mm, that far! I realised he was still very much a local saint, which I thought a shame given the provenance and uniqueness.

Of course the church was dedicated to St Oswald and St Edmund, and one of the other priests reminded me of the importance of Oswald in this area. Once again, the same people seem to crop up in other places, for this is the same King Oswald we came across at Holy Island. This seemed a long way from there, but then we knew that Oswald's Kingdom of Northumberland was huge. His presence is well recorded in Lancashire and Cheshire. Seemingly, Oswald was very fond of this part of his kingdom, around Ashton-in-Makerfield and further south to the small village of Winwick. History tells us that he died fighting the pagan Mercian King Penda in AD 642. Records state that he died at the Battle of Makerfield. This area of Lancashire claims the battle was here, though another town in Shropshire disputes this, but the link with Oswald here is strong.

Winwick is still a small, pretty village, but one which is struggling to maintain its separateness from the town of Warrington, which is continually expanding its boundaries. On a rise in the centre of the village is another St Oswald's Church, grade-1 listed and of great historic and architectural importance. A short way from the church is St Oswald's Well, which sprang up from the ground where he lay slain from the battle, and over time this spring was endowed with healing powers and attracted pilgrims. A further reminder of St Edmund and his family, the Gerards, can be found back in Winwick Church. Their family vault lies here, along with a famous brass which memorialises an earlier member of Edmund's family. This was Piers Gerard Esquire, who died on 19 June 1492.

Piers married into the famous powerful Stanley family, whose base was in both Cheshire and Lancashire, and they were a prominent family not just in the North, but in Britain as a whole. Piers' memorial brass is said to be one of the finest in England.

Whilst learning about Winwick, I came across another interesting story, that of the Great Broad Oak. This was a huge and wonderful specimen of an ancient oak tree, which in 1844 was said to cover an area of ground over 100 yards in circumference. The girth of its trunk was fourteen feet at its base, and the spread of its branches was so great that it served as a canopy for a huge special meal seating 124 people. Sadly the tree was blown down in 1850, and it must have been quite some storm to tumble such a huge tree.

There have been so many surprises for us in our native Lancashire. Once again we had had a good day, feeling we had experienced something special; an archaic ritual, but still so closely linked with an historical event of over 400 years ago, a spiritual tradition which in all these centuries has not changed at all.

The lovely interior of St Edmund's church.

Romanesque detail on church pillar.

Cross outside commemorating the Gerard family of Bryn, and Edmund's family.

ST NINIAN, SCOTLAND'S EARLY SAINT: ST NINIAN AT WHITHORN

We have heard of the Ruthwell Cross in other chapters of this book, a rightly famed sandstone cross of great beauty. Today Malc and I were seeing it in situ in the village church at Ruthwell, a few hundred yards from the Solway coast, which at this point consists mostly of mudflats and creeks, part of the estuary of the Rivers Esk, Sark and Kirtle Water, and English River Eden. From here it is but a short distance across to England. The coastal mountains of Cumbria are easily visible, with Skiddaw being the highest point. A cluster of typical terraced Galloway cottages comprises the village, sitting on the flat estuarial land. The church with its unusual square-shaped interior lies a bit further inland. It is an unprepossessing place to find such a wonderful eighth-century Anglian cross. Today it sits in a specially hollowed-out space which enables you to have a clear sight of this tall, stately sculpture, with its impressive carving, partly biblical and also comprising scrolls, patterns and leaves all entwined into a visually beautiful whole. It has not always rested here. For many years it lay broken and abandoned, and it is in relatively recent times that it was recovered and repaired.

We have made a purposeful visit here, but in fact this cross is only one of many stretching down this coast, leading to the pilgrim shine of St Ninian. Many have been lost, but a remarkable number still remain, including in the grounds of

Monreith House, the childhood home of Gavin Maxwell, the author famous for his book about otters, *Ring of Bright Water*.

Pilgrims from these distant times may already have experienced a long journey, and even on reaching Ruthwell they still had a very long way to go. The large number of crosses helped these pilgrims find their way. They were markers, prayer stops and meeting places, necessary in a remote area with few if any proper roads, much of it marsh, bog, forest and mountain. Yet to reach St Ninian's shrine at Whithorn seemed worth the long, hard, tiring journey.

The popularity of Iona means that many people associate St Columba with the first and major Christianising influence in Scotland. Yet, in fact, this accolade goes instead to St Ninian, who in the fifth century trod a lonely furrow in the remote Whithorn Peninsula in South-West Scotland. From this unlikely spot Ninian evangelised, and with his missionary zeal began Scotland's first conversion of those living in these remote corners of Scotland and of the North British residents of Cumbria.

Very little is known about Ninian, but he is thought to have been of noble birth, originating in this area and therefore having detailed knowledge of it. We know he became a priest and may have visited or even trained in Rome. What is certainly documented is that a church was already established here at Whithorn in the fifth century. We know this because Bede writes of him, telling us not only of the church but that it was built of stone – a very unusual practice in these Dark Ages, when most structures would have been of wood. More impressive too, the stone was white, the church being known as Candida Casa, the White Church, because of the light stone of its construction; it may have been modelled on one Ninian came across in his European travels. He was not part of the developing Celtic/Saxon Church as Hilda and Cuthbert were, but was almost certainly a priest of the Roman Catholic Church.

His base in this far-flung corner of Scotland was Whithorn, and despite its remoteness, his reputation and his ability to convert people to the Christian faith grew and the town developed. From the single small church, a priory and cathedral were established, becoming the focus for pilgrims, and the site became one of the most popular in Scotland for hundreds of years. Like many missionaries in these times, Ninian was a lover of solitude and he would retreat to what is now known as Ninian's Cave, north of Whithorn with a rocky access from a beach. The cave is accessible at low tide, involving a scramble across the rocks or across country. This bare, basic cave, damp and cold, still has crosses carved into the wall.

The priory and cathedral are now in a ruinous state, but today a visitor centre tells its story. A series of archaeological digs at the site have been remarkable, adding greatly to the knowledge of the site and of who and when people lived here.

The Whithorn Peninsula is only one of many varied landscapes found in Dumfries and Galloway, of which Whithorn is part. Most tourists travelling to Scotland miss this area altogether, passing Gretna and heading on up to the islands and Highlands. But if, instead, you turn left at Gretna on to the A75, a huge vista of beautiful countryside unfolds, changing along its route to Stranraer over a hundred miles away. Often said to be Scotland in miniature, it does indeed comprise all the elements found throughout Scotland as a whole. The peninsula where you find Whithorn is an area of undulating flatland with mud and salt flats, which today provide rich cattle grazing, with salt-marsh-grazed sheep and cows giving the meat an unusually tender and sweet flavour. In Ninian's time it was an inhospitable landscape of bog and marsh with specialist plants and flowers, including tough, resilient grass. It is windy and there are few trees.

In the next peninsula, known as the Rhins, is the small town of Portpatrick with an old port and quiet, attractive harbour. Yet, in former times this was the main port for trading links to Ireland and hence was a much busier place. Today that link is maintained by the daily ferry between Stranraer and Belfast, carrying on a centuries-old tradition. Portpatrick's importance is understandable; on a clear day Ireland can be seen very clearly across the Irish Sea. So close it seems that legend tells that St Patrick himself jumped from here across to Ireland. Outside its small harbour the sea can be extremely rough, in spite of the fact that this part of South-West Scotland has an exceptionally mild climate, where frost and snow are uncommon and where botanic and other show gardens grow exotic trees and plants which will not grow elsewhere.

There was also another trading commodity for which Portpatrick was well known. Most people know the tradition of Gretna Green, famous for English couples unable to marry for various reasons coming for elopement to Scotland, where marriage laws were different. Vows were often taken over an anvil in the blacksmith's shop, some of these weddings dating from 1750. Today marriage at Gretna Green in the remaining blacksmith's shop and other venues is still popular. It is seen still as a romantic place with so much history. What few people know is that although Gretna Green was by far the most important, Portpatrick was another 'marriage town', catering mainly for couples from Ireland seeking to marry in secret and in haste. Marriage was carried out very quickly here, with witnesses from the town readily available. However, blacksmiths did not conduct the marriages here. Rather, they were conducted by the local minister from the kirk. It was not a practice favoured by the locals, most of whom were strict Presbyterians of the Church of Scotland. However, the minister ignored the opposition, especially as this was a lucrative trade. Along with the volunteer witnesses, a few others assisted in various ways, and money was easily made, resulting from the high cost of marrying. Since many of the couples were from wealthy families, the local minister who presided at the events made far more money from these irregular marriages than he could ever make from his ministerial stipend. Where couples were able to avoid being caught by following relatives and dragged protestingly back home, then within twenty-four hours they would be back on the boat to Ireland, the elopement complete.

The importance and dependence on the sea for travel enabled

people to make journeys, such as Ireland to Portpatrick, easy, and this reliance on the sea was equally if not more important in the Dark Ages of Ninian. Without proper roads and maps, people generally travelled by water, and to the people to whom Ninian preached Whithorn would not seem to be remote. From both sides of the Solway up to Strathclyde, even down to the Lancashire and Cumbria coasts, people would sail without concern to Ninian's town; they knew the sea well. Further around the Whithorn Peninsula are other small now ruined chapels, overlooking small bays and beaches, built for the pilgrims to rest and pray after their sea journey. But pilgrims came from different directions too, and many did come by land, facing the long, gruelling journey, hazardous and uncomfortable, but clearly worth it when reaching journey's end.

On the other side of Dumfries, heading north, there is a pub with lovely unusual architectural details. This is the Auldgirth Inn, in the small village of Auldgirth. It is set back, but fronts the A76 – the main road to Ayr. The inn has characteristic arched windows and painted crosses decorating the roof and chimneys. It looks like an old chapel, and this observation makes sense when noting that the inn was possibly once a resting place for pilgrims on their way to Whithorn.

At Ruthwell we were on the same pilgrim path, but still many miles from Whithorn – journey's end. We hugged the Solway coast much of the way, passing river estuaries, mountains, large forests, small towns and tourist centres, much not having changed over many years, although people have made their mark in many ways. Nevertheless, the views and landmarks were very much the same as the pilgrims of old would have seen. This whole area was of politically strategic importance and, being the borderlands, many battles, incursions and thwarted invasions took place here on the edges of England and Scotland. Yes, it is physically remote, but people knew of it.

Edward I, called Longshanks, made a bid to claim Scotland. There was no bridge across the Anglo-Scottish boundary, so

Edward, like all other travellers, needed to cross the estuary by foot. This was dangerous: the tides are treacherous, as is the mud and sinking sand. There were a few safe crossing places and Edward stayed on the other side of the Solway at Burgh by Sands, waiting until the right time for him and his invading army to cross. Edward Longshanks never made this crossing. He died on the salt flats and his body was brought back and laid in the village church of Burgh by Sands, an unusual occurrence for a king.

Ninian lived a very long time ago and it would be easy to imagine that over the centuries he would be forgotten. In fact, his reputation continued.

Malc and I are members of the international Richard III Society, its aim being to expand knowledge about Richard and his time. Also, many members seek to improve and revise his image. He has possibly the most terrible image of any king and has been vilified and hated since Shakespeare wrote his play *Richard III*, portraying him as a vile, evil, murderous, hunchback king. Shakespeare believed this was a true picture and it is hard to change this image of him. However, there are many other aspects of this much maligned king which show Shakespeare to have been wrong, or at least swayed by public opinion in Tudor times. Richard, like most people of his time, in the fifteenth century, was a devoutly religious man, and a regular worshipper. Like many royal and noble people, Richard had his own book of hours, his own personal prayer book, which he carried with him on his travels. Before any battle, skirmish or other difficult situation, Richard, like everyone else, would pray; he would attend Mass before battle commenced. We know he had a priest say Mass before the Battle of Bosworth in 1485, where he lost his life. In this book of hours we find that he had adopted Ninian as his personal saint, the person he would call on during his prayers. Many have asked how could he have even known about Ninian? And indeed it does seem unlikely that a great English king centred on London and Northern England would know of such an early saint in the Scottish wilds. It is, however, very possible he knew of Ninian. He knew and visited Scotland; Carlisle Castle was his and Carlisle is not very far distant, just across the Solway. The Scottish branch of the Richard III Society felt it was important to recognise this link, both with Ninian and Scotland, and an information board about the link now stands in the Whithorn visitor centre, another historic link with an important and historic place.

As we continued our journey down we visited some more crosses, the Kilmorie Crosses. These are now covered and protected under glass, but they are a beautiful collection of crosses. Alas, of course, these days, these crosses no longer have a role in guiding pilgrims along their path. With signs, maps, guidebooks and satnav, Whithorn today is easy to find. However, the landscape is such that it's still possible to visualise the long pilgrim route with all its difficulties, and still capturing the excitement of these pilgrims as they reached the end of their arduous journey.

Driving back, we saw yet more examples of the beautiful Solway coast, an area of outstanding natural beauty, where at all times, but especially in autumn and winter, thousands upon thousands of geese and swans gather, having flown here for the winter. They feed on the many waterlogged fields and open water, characteristic of this marshy and muddy area. It is a wonderful thing at sunset to first hear the raucous sound of thousands of geese and, looking up, to see them in an often ragged V formation heading to a reserve for the night, flying in a sky turning pink, peach, purple and orange as the sun sets across the water, reflecting on the sea itself, a spectacle to remember.

Then out in the water at other times you can also see a strange line of fishermen just standing up to their chests in freezing cold water. These are the Ha'af Net fishermen, a fishing practice unique to the Solway Firth. Standing in the main channel they hold a stake in each hand, stretched wide, with netting in between. Here they stand for several hours, and not always in calm seas, waiting for the salmon swimming upriver. With some luck, the salmon swim into the netting, becoming trapped and hence caught. This method is an ancient one, a dangerous and skilful one, closely monitored and declining at a great rate. It would be very sad if it ceased altogether. A unique craft would be lost; a tradition, maybe even old enough for Ninian and the pilgrims to have seen it too!

> "For God so loved the world that he gave his only Son, that whoever believes in him should ... have eternal life."

VENERATING THE TRUE CROSS

Our frequent travels up and down the M6 take us past a landmark, always familiar and loved, not just by exiles like us, but by many Lancastrians. This is Winter Hill, forming part of the Pennine Hill Range, including Pendle Hill, further to the east and famous as witch country. Closer to and slightly to the side of Winter Hill is Rivington Pike, a beacon which, like many others across Britain, is lit on special occasions. This area around Rivington is a public country park, managed today by North West Water as reservoirs close by at Anglezarke provide drinking water. As a whole it is an expanse of moorland with pretty stone villages and provides miles of lovely walks.

Yet just over a century ago much of this land was owned by the entrepreneur and soap magnate Lord Lever, and parts are still called Lever Park. His legacy of Lever Brothers is still a successful international company. In his lifetime he was recognised as a follower of the garden-city movement and built his factory in a purpose-built village in the garden-city movement style for his workers. Named after his major product Sunlight Soap, this village is in the Wirral, part of Cheshire on a peninsula, much of which is coastal. This village of Port Sunlight is still a beautiful study in mixed architecture with houses and leisure facilities, which his workers would never have been able to afford to live in under normal circumstances. Today it has its own charm and is well worth a visit, especially the Port Sunlight Gallery of Lord Lever's art collection, which includes notable Pre-Raphaelite pictures.

But his heart was in another part of Lancashire; born in Bolton, to the south-east of Rivington, to a middle-class family in what was essentially a relatively poor working-class mill town, Lever loved the area, including the moorland around Rivington which he bought, and here he built his home. He built high on the moor and created unusual gardens too, including a folly in the form of a ruined castle and also Chinese gardens with their many rhododendrons. The house and most of the gardens have now been lost, reclaimed by nature, but there are still remnants hinting enigmatically of earlier times. In the house he built here, he maintained his lifelong habit of sleeping in the open air, which he did for most of his adult life. Pictures show his bedroom on an open terrace attached to the house. It was an eccentric trait which he continued even after his beloved wife, who shared his outdoor bed, died of pneumonia. Other photographs show the terrace room with minimal shelter, wet through after heavy showers. Rivington was only a short walk away from his home.

Today Rivington Pike, standing a short distance away, is still as popular and lovely as in Lord Lever's time, and it has become a tradition to walk up to the Pike over the Easter period, and especially on Good Friday. Many still uphold this tradition and there is a steady stream of visitors who come to tackle the climb in fair weather or foul. They are rewarded by taking refreshment in the valley in one of two enormous Saxon tithe barns, wonderful survivors, beautiful and evocative.

Just a few miles away is the town of Chorley, between Bolton and Preston. Originally a market town on a trade route along what is now the A6, Chorley is trying to maintain its image as a market town, but its designation as a new town some decades ago has meant considerable growth, creating a very different place. The town looks up to Chorley Nab, a rocky promontory, again part of the Pennine chain and linked to Rivington, along waymarked paths. Close to the base of the Nab in the older urban Chorley, in a street of unassuming Victorian terraces, lies another venue for an equally long Easter tradition. On this ordinary street is the extraordinary and beautiful Catholic Church of the Sacred Heart. This church holds a relic of the 'True Cross'. For 364 days this precious church relic is stored away. But on Good Friday it is brought out to be shown to worshippers in the church. It most certainly understates this event.

Trying to find details so Malc and I could attend, we searched for the relevant information. There was not even a mention of the relic, nor the expected veneration over Easter. We smiled when it vaguely told us that there is usually a service on Good Friday at 3 p.m. So did this mean that they no longer had the relic or no longer venerated it even if they had it? Or had I looked at the wrong relic in the wrong church in the wrong place? I always think there is nothing better than speaking to an actual person, so I picked up the phone to speak to the priest. It was a church helper who answered, and he was able to give me the information. Yes, they would be bringing in the piece of the 'True Cross' at the 3 p.m. service and again at 7 p.m. It was low-key to an extreme, though I had a lovely chat with the volunteer, with his clear Chorley accent which reminded me of home.

"Oh, I can tell where you are from," I said. "You sound so familiar."

"Everyone says that!" he replied. "I must have that particular voice and accent."

I later contemplated this seeming laid-back attitude. After all my research and visits, I now know that actual relics still in existence are extremely rare, and veneration even more so. But members of this urban Lancashire church probably do not see it this way. It is a ritual for this church and for its worshippers. No doubt they do not even think that anyone else would want to attend on Good Friday. So why would they publicise it, thinking there was no point? And in general their perception is probably true. There are not many people like me, who make special visits to such places today.

During the height of pilgrimage in the Middle Ages the situation could not have been more different. Then visiting many different sacred sites was one of the most popular activities.

Knowing this, churches and religious houses considered it essential that they should hold something which would attract pilgrims. It was considered something of a masterstroke to own a piece of the True Cross. Saints and relics were gloriously venerated, but the True Cross had an altogether different significance and a greater one. To see and even touch a piece of the Cross on which they believed Jesus had died brought people as close as they could be to a part of the physical Jesus and His life. It was an experience of great wonder, mystery and emotion, an insight into and realisation of the truth that Jesus really did die on the Cross; an act of salvation for all humankind who believe in Him. This promise of salvation through sacrifice was a truly holy experience.

Of course such a coup for a holy house meant not only pilgrims, but the gifts, great wealth and kudos arising from such a precious relic. The wish to own such a relic was therefore not only wishful, but indeed essential. Of course greed was often an unpleasant outcome, leading to corruption and malpractice within the Church.

Yet this did not deter the pilgrims, and at the height of such venerations thousands of churches across Europe claimed to hold a piece of the True Cross.

Many people have commented that if all these claims were added together, then the wood comprising these parts of the Cross would probably be enough to fill a forest; an exaggeration, but the reasoning behind the saying has more than a basis of truth. There is probably no doubt that many, perhaps even the vast majority, of the 'True Cross' fragments were fake, and it is hard to understand from a modern perspective how so many people over so many centuries believed these relics to be genuine. However, the pilgrims didn't live in our times, and yet they weren't necessarily overly naive. Rather, their faith was strong. It was an intrinsic and vital part of their lives, and the idea that the 'True Cross' they revered and glorified was not genuine would not have occurred to them. They wanted to believe! And of course it was, after all, a small piece of wood. How could it be proved by looking at it whether or not it was authentic? By the same argument, how could people have denied it was the real thing? To see the relic was to bring the pilgrim into the closest possible relationship to Jesus. It was a real physical reminder of His death on the Cross, far away in a country of which they had no real conception. More importantly, Jesus promised them redemption and salvation.

These pilgrims, along with Britain's general population, needed to believe in this salvation, for such was their fear of not entering heaven, and indeed accepting the certain reality of hell, that they would try many ways to ensure they were not deemed sinful and unworthy of a place in heaven.

The act of veneration in a small-town Catholic church of a fragment of the 'True Cross' is not something happening centuries ago, but today. To me, whether or not it is authentic is almost irrelevant. It is an extremely long-held tradition and no doubt is undertaken as it always has been. I am sure that some members of the congregation simply see it as upholding a tradition. Others may venerate what they consider to be a real representation of the Cross, with its vital message for Christians the world over. It is an event which unifies all Christians on the saddest of days. Then there must still be those who, even today, believe that this piece of wood truly is a part of the Cross on which Jesus was crucified, a remaining element from the Cross on which Jesus suffered an agonising and humiliating death. And really who are we modern Britons, many sceptical, to pour scorn on these believers? Despite the thousands of fakes, might there have been those which really were what they claimed to be: wood from Jesus's tree of Crucifixion, imbued with His suffering, His physical human agony, His love, and ultimately His transforming commitment to redeem, forgive, sanctify and fulfil His promise of eternal life. We can still recognise Him today, as those pilgrims of old did, as Our Lord and Saviour. Whatever our beliefs, Jesus really did sacrifice His life, and the Cross reminds us and communicates to us what it meant for Jesus and for us.

I saw that he is at work unceasingly in every conceivable thing and that it is all done so well, so wisely, and so powerfully that it is far greater than anything we can imagine, guess or think.

Mother Julian, Revelations of divine love.

St Julian of Norwich

TWO WOMEN OF NORFOLK: ST JULIAN OF NORWICH AND OUR LADY OF WALSINGHAM

From our home in Scotland this proved to be the longest of our journeys. After seven hours we are in Norwich. Even in these days of efficient road networks, East Anglia still remains an area in itself, still geographically remote from the country's main arterial road network. Yet Norfolk's history is profound, early and important, being one of the earliest occupied and developed parts of the UK. But the access by sea was far more important than by land. As 'northerners' we are used to some prejudicial comments about us from our southern neighbours. Yet we can have our little prejudices too. I have to admit that Norfolk is not somewhere I would normally choose to visit. We like our hills up north, and East Anglia is . . . well, flat! However, we can all revise our opinions and both Malc and I came to love Norwich and Norfolk.

I had come here to find the pilgrimage sites of two amazing women: St Julian of Norwich and Richeldis de Faverches, more fondly known as Our Lady of Walsingham. For this visit, we were joined by another intrepid traveller as my friend Alison joined us in Norwich for a couple of days, so I was again reminded of my student days, as Alison and I were house sharers in Coventry when we were both undergraduates. Alison is from Hertfordshire, now living in Essex. We don't see each other often and it was lovely to combine my pilgrimage with a little reunion. We both lived in a lovely big student house on Kenilworth Road with a men's student house around the corner, very convenient! Whoever the original owners were they had lots of money, but sadly, by the time students occupied it the tennis courts and swimming pool were out of action. But it was still a wonderful party house, and these were held at every opportunity. One I remember clearly was a tramps party, and my mum made me an outfit out of an old jute sack! It seems very fitting now as I continue my pilgrimages. I have had the sackcloth, but not the ashes! Sorry! Coventry when we were students was often a target or threatened target from the IRA, and bomb alerts at concerts, and on Saturdays in town-centre cafés, were common and we got used to them. When it came to our graduation ceremony, however, a bomb threat to the cathedral where it was to be held meant the whole ceremony was cancelled and never reorganised. Thirty-five years later I went back to Coventry when finally they had another ceremony for those who had never had the chance to receive their degree in a formal setting. I had later taken a Masters degree and so I decided it was not so important for me to take part officially, but it was a wonderful occasion being back there and strolling around all the familiar places. The event also captured the imagination of both TV and newspapers, in which Alison and I both featured. Not many graduates have to wait thirty-five years before receiving their degree! Is that a record?

But back to Norwich, where there seemed so much to see and do, but I managed to stay focused on my tasks. We were able to stay right in the heart of the city in an area called Tomb Land in a hotel dating from the thirteenth century, which was right opposite Norwich's huge cathedral, as well as being convenient to explore the city on foot. Our hotel had seen many changes and additions over time, which gave it character and lots of nooks and crannies. The hotel manager told us that in all there are actually thirteen different buildings, all melded somehow into one.

It was possibly my interest in Julian of Norwich which first prompted me to do my many pilgrimages. I had known of her for several years and use her readings both privately and in my worship services. Julian lived in the 1300s and with her book *Revelations of Divine Love* she was the first woman to write a book in English. This in itself is a reason to read her works, but equally and possibly more important is the fact that her religious interpretations seem so far ahead of her time, as well as being uplifting and comforting. She was a remarkable woman and astonishing in her wisdom and serenity. In her early thirties, Julian became an anchorite within the church of St Julian in Norwich, so it was to this church we went in search of her. I didn't know what to expect, but what I saw was something of a surprise. Rather than imposing, the church was small, built of flint and tucked away down an alley opposite what would have been in her time a busy place across from the harbour and port on the River Wensum. I suppose I expected an impressive church; it wasn't, but it was a lovely church nonetheless. Prior to her becoming an anchorite, Julian was so ill that she contemplated her own death and was given the last rites. At this crucial moment she received a series of visions of Jesus and Mary. It was as a result of these that she devoted herself to Jesus. She had been saved from death at a vital moment and had no doubt she was intended to receive and interpret these visions for the benefit of all Christians. These visions gave her an insight into the nature of God and His purpose. She knew that she had to spend years in contemplation to understand and then communicate these messages from God, and indeed it did take her many years to finally understand them, during which time she wrote down what she believed to be God's meaning.

The church was small, quiet, peaceful and unassuming, but with some lovely old artefacts, including a fourteenth-century stone font with exquisite crisp carvings of saints around its perimeter. To the side of the church, off the nave but separate from it, is St Julian's Cell. As we were looking around the lights came on and Shirley, a 'Julian volunteer', joined us and told us many interesting facts about Julian and her life.

"The cell itself", she said, "has been rebuilt. It was destroyed by Henry VIII. Then during bombing in the Second World War, when clearing the land, the ground showed physical evidence of where the cell would have been. It has now been rebuilt, but one cannot say positively it is exactly the same. In fact, we know it is larger than the cell would actually have been and it may have been only half the present size – probably no more than eleven feet by ten."

It is impossible to really imagine it. But even today it has a feeling of serenity and peace. What must it have been like for her to live here though, in a self-imposed prison cell? Shirley told us that very little is known about Julian, not even being sure that this was her real name, although it was a popular name at the time.

Becoming an anchorite meant that she effectively became a recluse and no one undertook such a way of life without great thought. Indeed, and understandably, there were strict written rules and each potential anchorite had to be approved by the local bishop, having to prove they had a true understanding of the rules and possessed the character needed to literally and totally retreat from daily life. In addition, a potential anchorite had to prove they had enough money to sustain them and to afford a maid to look after them. Never leaving their anchorhold meant having no access to food or anything needed to sustain even the basics of life; so someone had to source and cook food for her, as well as provide water and clothes. The fact that Julian was able to do this probably indicates she was from a noble family, and the fact she could read and write supports this theory. After being accepted, Julian moved into her cell.

Shirley continued her story for us: "As she began her life as an anchorite, the Bishop and others present would perform a funeral service. This signalled the end of her former life. Effectively her life in the outside world had ended! Then, on entering her cell, about ten feet square, the door was bricked up and sealed for the next forty years until her death at around eighty years old."

Such a sobering thing to undertake. It is hard for anyone to imagine how she must have felt when she heard the door sealed up, never to open again until she died.

However, she was not totally cut off from people, as is evident by a small window which opened into the church and whereby she could hear the Mass. Also the area at the time, being close to the harbour and river, was probably a busy and noisy place, and no doubt she could hear many sounds of life outside. Julian was considered a wise woman and alongside her contemplation, prayer and writing she became well known in the area. Somewhere in her cell there must have been a small opening to the outside, but not a door – most likely at the side on to a small garden area. This gave locals and pilgrims some limited access to Julian. She was sought by thousands during her anchorite life. They came for solace in grief and despair, for prayer, forgiveness and understanding. Her advice and guidance were highly respected, and Julian herself knew what she did and said was valued and that God was pleased with her.

I have recently reread Anya Seton's great novel *Katherine*, considered by many to be one of the best if not the best historical novel ever written. I was surprised to read that Julian features in it. The story tells of the life of Katherine Swinford, who was the mistress and later the wife of John of Gaunt, Duke of Lancaster. Like many people in times of crisis we see Katherine seeking advice and consolation from Julian. It may or may not be true, of course, but Katherine was a real person who lived for many years in Lincolnshire. She had a deep faith and she would certainly have known of her. And of course people still seek out her words and visit today. Shirley confirmed that people come from all over the world. Many schoolchildren use Julian's work to study medieval writing, and many of those who come not knowing anything at all about her do, I feel sure, leave acknowledging she was a brave and wonderful woman. Hopefully too, her deep faith, her life and understanding of the nature of God will also have a lasting influence on visitors. Others are deeply familiar with her writings. Many visit often, and may become 'friends', whose role is to continue to follow Julian's teaching and also to ensure that Julian and her importance to Christianity are not forgotten.

I was surprised to discover that there were many anchorites in Julian's time and especially in Norwich and Norfolk. Yet it is Julian who is mostly remembered. She left behind a body of written work which is as valuable and meaningful today as it was in the fourteenth century, as well as being spiritually uplifting. The life of an anchorite is not just something we can say is difficult. It seems to me that it is something so hard to understand – how anyone would cope with such an undertaking, not just for years, but for decades. We have so little information about Julian the woman, and yet tradition passed down tells us that Julian was happy in her confinement. The rules she had to maintain as an anchorite were harsh, and these were on top of enclosure. We do know though that Julian had a cat of her own as a pet. Being deprived of the sense of touch which we take for granted on meeting people, must have seemed like true isolation to anchorites. The softness afforded by stroking her cat must have been a comfort to her. We forget when not deprived of it that touch is a vital sensory need. On a practical level, her cat was also useful for catching vermin.

"Being so close to the port", Shirley told us, "meant that rats and mice were prevalent."

As I left the church my feelings for Julian were profound, and actually seeing where and how she lived had brought her closer. My respect and admiration for her are great. I felt uplifted and also felt small in the shadow of such a courageous woman, who devoted totally her life to Jesus. How many of us would even contemplate this today, let alone do it?

I saw that he is at work unceasingly in every conceivable thing, and that it is all done so well, so wisely, and so powerfully, that it is far greater than anything we can imagine, guess or think.

Mother Julien, Revelations of divine love.

Norwich has a lovely river, the Wensum, with paths perfect for strolling and bordered by many beautiful mature weeping willows. The river also gives access to the close and cathedral. During Julian's time this must have been a very different place, the cathedral newly built and the river busy with wherries plying up and down along the inland rivers and up to the port at Norwich, far from the coast. It must've been a bustling place, a wealthy place with wool exported in vast quantities to the continent, its revenue making merchants rich and able to pay for the building of Norfolk's beautiful large churches, another way in which rich people felt able to buy favour with God. Part of this former riverside area is now being gentrified and redeveloped, with a new bridge named after Julian spanning the river, close to where she lived. Comprising a retail park, a leisure area and new apartments, it may not be everyone's idea of redevelopment, but it certainly gives the impression that Norwich is flourishing. Yet the old city has not been lost, being a city of closes and narrow streets. There are still many old houses in and around the river and cathedral areas, often tucked away, quiet, with cottage gardens, their appearance seemingly more like country cottages, away from the city bustle and yet at the heart of it.

Norwich is also a place of churches, as is Norfolk as a whole. Local flint gives them character. What are often called the 'wool churches' can be large and impressive. Some of the flint decoration is beautifully napped and shines like obsidian. In Norwich, many like that of Julian are tucked away in hidden corners, some now used for things other than worship.

My friend Alison said that the last time she visited Norwich she went to the Colman's Mustard Shop, but we looked and it was impossible to find. Of course the city is famous for its mustard, but on asking the hotel manager for information he said the shop was closed and was unlikely to reopen. Even worse, it seemed there is a campaign to keep open the factory itself, not just its shop. Now owned by Unilever, it is threatened with closure and Unilever is less than popular in the area! I later read about it in the local paper, which was spearheading the campaign. They were asking Norwich City football supporters for the next match to dig out their old football kits from the time when Colman's sponsored the team. Amazingly, by digging deep into the backs of cupboards and attics, hundreds of fans turned up in these old shirts in protest! The probability, though, is that the factory will close. It isn't easy to fight a multinational company like Unilever! Such a shame, though, the city will probably end up with a museum recalling the heyday of Colman's mustard!

Walsingham pilgrimage church.

It was time for another journey, this time heading north towards the coast to the small village of Walsingham, just a few miles from Norwich. The village is comprised of small streets of townhouses, remarkably unchanged and unspoilt despite centuries of pilgrims whose feet have tramped endlessly up and down these small streets. When we visited it was a damp mild day and quiet.

Richeldis de Faverches was a noblewoman, wife of a large landowner who lived in the area of Walsingham in the eleventh century. One day she experienced a vision of Mary, mother of Jesus. This was one of the first records of such visions, and in her vision Richeldis found herself with Mary's guidance transported to Nazareth to the house where Mary had lived. The vision was of a simple square box of a house. As we now know this was the typical type of house in the country where Jesus lived, square with mud walls, and a flat roof used very much as another room. Mary indicated to Richeldis that she would like her to recreate such a house at Walsingham. She went on to build a simple wooden structure, and where a stream and well emerged at its side proving to have health and curing benefits. Richeldis heard Mary say, "Those who seek me there will find succour." This small, simple building came to represent England's Nazareth, developing rapidly into a centre of Marian focus, especially for women seeking pregnancy. Pilgrims soon started to flock to England's Nazareth and it quickly became part of the pilgrim round. Pilgrimage was becoming a very in thing to do, as Crusades with their Christian verve to free Jerusalem fired the imagination of many. It would have been the ambition of most to travel to the Holy Land, particularly Jerusalem, Bethlehem and Nazareth. What could be better than to visit the actual place where Jesus lived? And thousands did go. But for most people it just wasn't possible. The establishment of the 'Nazareth House' therefore became an alternative. Of course it wasn't Mary's house, but it was as she would have lived. They learned what houses in the Holy Land were like, squat, square, simply built and with flat roofs. Pilgrims could associate with it and they knew it was the closest they would ever get to the Holy Land. In addition there were wells and streams reputed to have healing properties.

Like so many other spiritual buildings, the Nazareth House was destroyed by Henry VIII, in 1538. However, the springs and wells remained, and people still came to seek healing; and it is said that thousands were healed. After its destruction, Walsingham could have passed into obscurity, but for the intervention and determination of one man. The man was Father Alfred Hope Patten. He rebuilt the shrine in 1931, and in many ways it copies the former, reflecting features which the pilgrims of old would have recognised. Walsingham has developed and flourished from this time and pilgrims continue to flock here. The site is not overly spacious, much of it taken up by new retreats and training buildings, a small exhibition area and a café. A peaceful landscaped garden is laid out with Stations of the Cross and then dominating the further end is the church within which the rebuilt Nazareth House resides: a separate but intrinsic part of the whole church assemblage. Services are held here every day. It is a living and breathing testimony to modern Christianity, with its emphasis on pilgrimage, meditation, retreat, peace and the presence of God. And the Nazareth House of Mary is a permanent link between the faith of today and the land and people of Jesus's time and country.

Malc and I attended a 'sprinkling' service in the shrine church. The resident priest conducted a short service and then we were led to the well, which was at a slightly lower level than the church and was one of the wells rediscovered when the church was rebuilt. This well never runs dry. Firstly, we were given this 'holy water' to drink, then the priest signed a cross on our foreheads with the water as a blessing, and then finally we had water poured on to our hands; a healing flow of water. There were probably about fifteen of us altogether and we all partook, holding some of the flowing water in our hands. The woman in front of us, we noticed, sprayed the holy water on to her spine. Malc rubbed his on to his heart and thumb joint. I sprinkled my drops on to both my stomach and my arthritic knee, which needs to be replaced. It was a really peaceful, pleasant and sacred experience, and I can understand its popularity amongst those distant as well as today's pilgrims.

We then visited the Holy House. Incorporated inside the church, it really is a box-like structure with an altar and a lovely statue of Mary and Jesus. The whole was surrounded by rows of shelves full of burning candles and votives in an area set apart for prayer and meditation.

As I have journeyed around to these pilgrimage sites I have been surprised how many linkages there are between them. Here were more links. Probably the most popular pilgrimage enshrined in history, described by Geoffrey Chaucer in his *Canterbury Tales*, was to the tomb of St Thomas à Becket in Canterbury. Today there is no shrine or any evidence at all of Thomas à Becket there. His shrine, an unusual foramina shrine, was destroyed not by Henry VIII, but presumably by his powerful acolyte Thomas Cromwell. His fervent Protestantism encouraged playwright John Bale to write plays which then incensed the public, resulting in the destruction of Thomas à Becket's tomb and shrine around 1538. Today, only a candle remains, lit daily in the cathedral at the spot where Becket's shrine stood. Yet, at Walsingham, there are what are said to be some remains of Thomas à Becket, held in a small wooden painted box. Maybe St Thomas à Becket is not completely lost after all.

Outside we came across another beautiful little chapel, the Chapel of All Souls, dedicated to the dead and dying. Although seemingly slightly macabre, it is in fact a chapel of peace and tranquillity with some lovely stained glass. Inside I spoke to Janet Hand. She was on a three-day pilgrimage, having travelled with a church group from Brighton, and it was not her first visit. Janet's husband, she told us, died the previous year and this sad event had prompted her to return to find time to remember and pray for him in a chapel built exactly for that purpose.

In the exhibition area back at the main entrance, where we learned more about Our Lady of Walsingham, we also spoke to a volunteer, Tim. His role, amongst others, was to welcome people. He told me he lived locally now, but was originally from Oxford. He openly explained about changes to his life.

"I had visited here several times," he told us. "When my wife died and my circumstances totally changed, I decided to move here and now share a house with my cousin, who is also a volunteer here."

Continuing our conversation, I asked him, "How many visitors and pilgrims come to Walsingham?"

"There are main events, two or three times a year, when thousands of people come."

It clearly remains a popular place and is purpose-built for its pilgrims.

We had time left to stroll around the village and visit the shrine shop. Then it was back to Norwich. We saw the sign for the Slipper Chapel about a mile out of town, which we unfortunately didn't manage to see. This is a Roman Catholic chapel, and in days past pilgrims walked barefoot from the Slipper Chapel the mile to the actual shrine.

We had had an inspiring and meditative day. Walsingham remains a popular place of pilgrimage for many Christians, and I can understand why people come here. Yet I have to admit that I much preferred St Julian's Cell with its simplicity and sense of true devotion and love of God. Julian, I feel, has much more to say about the nature of Our Lord, and even after 700 years we can still learn from her words, which are as relevant today as ever. It is where I would go back to.

And here comes another coincidence. At the time of our visit there were some changes afoot with the Julian Centre, quite momentous and sad changes. For many years the Julian Fellowship and guest house had been closely supported and run by a small community of nuns, the Sisters of the Community of All Hallows. Prominent amongst the sisters was Sister Pamela, whom I didn't meet but who was spoken of fondly. The sisters had sadly accepted the fact that as only four remained in the community it was felt it was no longer able to maintain itself. The community was to disperse and the sisters after so many years together were separated and moved on, out and outward, into new ministries.

It was only some months later that through my Friends of Julian newsletter I learned that Sister Pamela had actually decided to move to the Iona Community (in fact Mull as I found out later). As Iona was a major part of my pilgrimage journeys this seemed a strange coincidence. I have since contacted her and she appears again in my narrative in my Iona pilgrimage journey.

On our last morning we said farewell to Alison, but we still had a little time to look around Norwich. Just opposite our hotel was one of Norwich's more famous and lovely old streets, Elmhill. Considered one of the oldest and most picturesque streets, we strolled to the top and noticed a speciality – The Teddy Bear Shop. I thought it a perfect opportunity to look for a take-home gift for my special niece and nephew. It was a splendid shop, but I quickly changed my mind about the gifts. This was no ordinary soft-toy shop. Rather, it was clearly a place for collectors of teddies and other soft toys. Many were unique and some were priced at £500. Not all were so expensive, but none were cheap. As lovely and special as they are, my niece and nephew would not be getting one. Malc and I made a rather hurried exit!

It was time for a cuppa and we walked a little further on into the heart of the shopping area and there found a lovely place called Harriet's. As a passionate tea drinker and hater of coffee, this café was a revelation; tea nirvana. As a traditional tea shop it did not serve coffee! No, none at all. Yay! Waitresses did not have 'barista' written on their backs. It was elegant and quiet. No supremely noisy coffee machines, loud enough sometimes to fry your brains and far too loud to engage in conversation with your companions. Yet they served upwards of twenty different teas, made silently by simply boiling the kettle and pouring water on to a pot of tea leaves. How simple and refined! And the café was full. I was impressed.

Then it was time to head home. It was, of course, another long journey and proved much busier than our first. Driving down, the weather had been very odd, quite spooky. The sky was dark, apparently caused by air saturated with desert sand. It was very warm and on the few occasions when the sun managed to break through the strange atmospheric dust it was like a huge blood orange hanging in the dark, menacing sky. It was how I imagine the Day of Judgement will be. On the return journey the weather was much more normal. Not being familiar with East Anglia, we neither of us expected each county to be so different. We found Lincolnshire to be most definitely flat. The fields were huge and stretched in infinite length. There were no verges, hedges or fences. Each field seemed to approach the very edge of the road. Nor did we expect wind turbines, but we realised that the very flatness of the land meant it was very windy. Indeed, we noticed how blustery it was and the wind turbines were flying around. It seemed too as if the trees didn't grow very tall, lacking large specimen trees and then in places looking rather like France, rows of poplars rising up and bowing in the wind. But the area did have its own character, with villages and church spires seemingly exposed and rising up out of the flat fields, the church spires tall and gracious. Norfolk, we found, was nothing like this. Although it was flat, it was heavily treed, so much so that the landscape didn't appear so flat. These trees of many different types seemed to break up the flat landscape, lending it an air of gentle contours.

Malc and I did allow ourselves a little northern joke, however. We could hardly believe it when on what the area considered to be a dangerously steep road, a crawler lane had been introduced for lorries and slower traffic!

"A crawler lane," we laughed. "Where's the hill? It's nothing but a slight slope. Come a bit further north, we'll show you some steep hills!"

Sorry, Norfolk and Lincolnshire, we did like your area – we did, honest. And indeed we did. We came home with some lovely memories and some enriching spiritual experiences. We are still monitoring the effects of the 'holy water'.

Inside Julian's Cell today, rebuilt after the Second World War.

Inside the Church of St Julian, the door to Julian of Norwich's cell. When she lived here, this door would have been sealed up.

The window from Julian's Cell which allowed her to listen to the Mass in the church beyond.

Fourteenth-century carved font at the entrance to St Julian's Church, Norwich.

Beautiful twentieth-century stained-glass window in Norwich Cathedral.

The small Church of St Julian, where Julian's Cell is found.

The healing well in the Church of Our lady of Walsingham in Norfolk, still used for healing on a daily basis.

REFLECTIONS

Twenty-two pilgrimages in a period of two and a half years proved a big undertaking, and yet I could have done a lot more; I just had to stop somewhere. I chose these particular ones because each one seemed different, with something interesting to offer. It was amazing just how much there was to see and learn.

It all began with me wanting to take on a personal odyssey, and why pilgrimage came to mind is a mystery. It just popped into my mind and somehow I knew it was what I was meant to do. Later I realised that other people might find my experiences both interesting and meaningful, so I decided to write them down, leading to this book.

The purpose is still unclear, and there were probably many reasons, some of which are hard to define. I love history, especially Saxon and medieval. I also wanted to explore the spiritual experiences of those who lived in different, and often challenging, times, perhaps trying to catch an echo of those fellow pilgrims as I trod the same paths. Certainly, it proved a good way of highlighting an interesting aspect of history, and also as a meaningful part of life today. There is no doubt that pilgrimage survives, even the idea of pilgrimage, presented as soul-searching and the seeking of meaning in our lives. In places it still thrives, as in Walsingham, a place at the forefront of continuing and growing pilgrim culture. Equally St Edmund Arrowsmith has a continuous history of veneration over hundreds of years, which goes on almost unnoticed by the world at large, in its small Lancashire enclave.

Pilgrimage and veneration are alive and well.

Like many people, my view of pilgrims was influenced by those we find in Chaucer's *Canterbury Tales*. Here we see mostly individual pilgrims travelling purposefully for what is hoped will lead to healing, forgiveness, intercession and thanks. In many instances this is a true reflection, as the number of 'relic shrines' testifies. But, from my own journeys, I was surprised how many sites didn't fit this pattern, for example, those of Ninian, Kentigern, Columba, Hilda, Cuthbert, Bertram, Bede and Julian. These people were visited as revered people in their own lifetimes. True, they were later proclaimed saints and were also found to have healing abilities, but it was pilgrimage to a living person which was of primary importance. These people were loved, revered and respected, and pilgrims valued their wisdom, advice, counsel, common sense and intelligence as well as their deep expression of faith. Then, as now, it was important to have people to trust, and who showed selflessness and, yes, goodness. People admired these qualities, and we still do.

In the end I felt privileged to have taken these journeys. Many sites have now passed into obscurity, totally destroyed or fallen into ruin, but in its heyday pilgrimage was an integral part of many people's lives. So many have fallen into disuse, but does this mean that soul-searching, spiritual enlightenment and pilgrimage is no longer relevant in our lives and society today? Probably the opposite is true. We still need those special places, and we also still need those special people, like those recognised by pilgrims over 1,000 years ago. It is still vital to have those 'right' role models, whose character and perhaps faith can help guide us through life, to face difficult times and to learn. Maybe we can be guided to a better place. As a Christian my perfect role model is Jesus. But for us all, with or without faith there is a need to journey, even if only in our minds, so we can seek the scallop shell of pilgrimage. Life itself is a pilgrimage, an opportunity to take those vital journeys, seeking many things, and where hopefully we will also *find*.

REFERENCES

1. *Peregrini Lindisfarne: An Anthology*
2. *The Secret History of the Knights Templar*, Susie Hodge
3. *Whitby Jet* (Shire Library), Helen and Katy Muller
4. *Golf: Strangest Tales*
5. Official guidebooks from:
   Hexham Abbey
   Whitby Abbey
   St Andrews
   Hereford Cathedral
   Shrewsbury Abbey
   Glasgow Cathedral
   Durham Cathedral
   Samye Ling Buddhist Centre
   St Fillans, Aberdour
   The Shrine of Our Lady of Walsingham
   Hereford Cathedral – stained glass
6. *Arthur and the Lost Kingdoms*, Alastair Moffat
7. *The Druids*, Stuart Piggott
8. *The Fury of the Northmen*, John Marsden
9. *The Durham Coalfield*
10. *Coal*
11. *Cuthbert and the Northumbrian Saints*, Paul Frodsham
12. *Chaucer*, Peter Ackroyd
13. *Revelations of Divine Love*, Julian of Norwich
14. *The Ecclesiastical History of the English People*, Bede

15. *Saint Andrew: Scotland's Myth and Identity*, Michael T. R. B. Turnbull
16. *The Pilgrim Journey: A History of Pilgrimage in the Western World*, James Harpur
17. *Pioneers of Scottish Christianity: Ninian, Columba and Mungo*, Roderick Graham
18. *Mull and Iona*, P. A. McNab
19. *The Canterbury Tales*, Geoffrey Chaucer